AF270322

The American Way of Foreign Policy

The American Way of Foreign Policy

Ideology, Economics, Democracy

MICHAEL MANDELBAUM

OXFORD
UNIVERSITY PRESS

Oxford University Press is a department of the University of Oxford.
It furthers the University's objective of excellence in research, scholarship,
and education by publishing worldwide. Oxford is a registered trade mark of
Oxford University Press in the UK and in certain other countries.

Published in the United States of America by Oxford University Press
198 Madison Avenue, New York, NY 10016, United States of America.

CIP data is on file at the Library of Congress

ISBN 9780197840931

DOI: 10.1093/oso/9780197840931.001.0001

Printed by Sheridan Books, Inc., United States of America

The manufacturer's authorized representative in the EU for product safety is
Oxford University Press España S.A. of Parque Empresarial San Fernando de Henares,
Avenida de Castilla, 2 – 28830 Madrid (www.oup.es/en or product.safety@oup.com).
OUP España S.A. also acts as importer into Spain of products made by the manufacturer.

ALSO BY MICHAEL MANDELBAUM

The Titans of the Twentieth Century: How They Made History and the History They Made (2024)

The Four Ages of American Foreign Policy: Weak Power, Great Power, Superpower, Hyperpower (2022)

The Rise and Fall of Peace on Earth (2019)

Mission Failure: America and the World in the Post–Cold War Era (2016)

The Road to Global Prosperity (2014)

That Used to Be Us: How America Fell Behind in the World It Invented and How We Can Come Back (with Thomas L. Friedman) (2011)

The Frugal Superpower: America's Global Leadership in a Cash-Strapped World (2010)

Democracy's Good Name: The Rise and Risks of the World's Most Popular Form of Government (2007)

The Case for Goliath: How America Acts as the World's Government in the Twenty-First Century (2006)

The Meaning of Sports: Why Americans Watch Baseball, Football, and Basketball and What They See When They Do (2004)

The Ideas That Conquered the World: Peace, Democracy and Free Markets in the Twenty-First Century (2002)

The Dawn of Peace in Europe (1996)

The Global Rivals (with Seweryn Bialer) (1996)

The Fate of Nations: The Search for National Security in the Nineteenth and Twentieth Centuries (1988)

Reagan and Gorbachev (with Strobe Talbott) (1987)

The Nuclear Future (1983)

The Nuclear Revolution: International Politics Before and After Hiroshima (1983)

The Nuclear Question: The United States and Nuclear Weapons, 1946–1976 (1979)

CONTENTS

ACKNOWLEDGMENTS

This book has an unusual history. The idea for it originated in a conversation I had in 2008 with Lai Thai Binh, who was then a student at the Johns Hopkins University School of Advanced International Studies (SAIS), where I taught. Now his country's ambassador to the Philippines, he had come to SAIS from the Vietnamese foreign ministry to learn about American foreign policy, the subject I was teaching. He asked me, "What should I read to understand the foreign policy of the United States?" I mentioned many books, articles, journals, magazines, and newspapers. He responded, "That's helpful, but is there one thing I can read that will give me a basic understanding of the subject?" I was stumped. I couldn't think of one. I continued to ponder his question long after the conversation had taken place and resolved to write a book that would give him and others what he had wanted.

When I began planning to write it, I realized that while I knew the history of American foreign policy after 1945 very well, and its history between 1898 and 1945 tolerably well, I did not know the eighteenth- and nineteenth-century history well enough to write the book I had in mind. In discussing with my wife the project on which I proposed to embark, I noted that in order to complete it successfully, I would have to learn the eighteenth- and nineteenth-century history of America's foreign relations. "In that case," she said, "why not write a history of all of American foreign policy?"

So I did.

That book, *The Four Ages of American Foreign Policy: Weak Power, Great Power, Superpower, Hyperpower*, was published in 2022 by Oxford University Press. It was not the book that I had initially intended to write, but writing it showed me how that intended book, the book that would provide the answer to Lai Binh's question, could be written. *The Four Ages* describes and analyzes its subject through four distinct historical periods, from 1765 to 2015, each of them defined by the relative power of the United States in the international system. That book also identifies three distinct and important features of American foreign policy that have persisted, and exerted major influence, from the eighteenth century to the twenty-first. Those three enduring features—the effects of political ideas, the use of economic instruments to achieve political goals, the pervasive influence of the public—their origins, the reasons that they are distinctly American, their appearance in four different centuries, and their impact on the United States and the world, are the subjects of *The American Way of Foreign Policy*.

In the course of writing this book, and of writing *The Four Ages* as well, I had many relevant and fruitful conversations with my friend Nicholas X. Rizopoulos, himself an accomplished diplomatic historian, for which I am most grateful.

Angela Chnapko and Lacey Harvey of Oxford University Press, and David McBride, now of Princeton University Press but recently at Oxford, were helpful in shepherding this book through the process that has culminated in publication.

My greatest debt, as with all the books I have written over the past fifty years, is to my wife, Anne Mandelbaum, who not only steered me on to the proper, albeit circuitous, literary path, but also made this book, as she has all the others I have written, clearer and more coherent than they would have been without her sensitive and characteristically punctilious editing.

Even more important, I am grateful for her peerless companionship, her great wit, her daily good cheer, and her extraordinary patience, insight, ingenuity, and kindness.

What is distinctively American about American foreign policy? How, that is, have the relations of the United States with other countries differed from the external relations of the other sovereign states in the international system over the 250 years since the thirteen North American colonies proclaimed their independence from Great Britain in 1776?

A long-standing intellectual and, in the United States, political tradition holds that in its *internal* affairs America has been and continues to be, distinctive. By this account, the absence, in North America, of the hierarchies that marked the societies of Europe—monarchies, landed aristocracies, a history of feudalism, and established churches—has shaped the politics, the culture, the social structure and the economic life of the United States in ways that have set it apart from the countries of the Old World.[1] These absences have, since the colonial era, underpinned what has come to be called "American exceptionalism." According to this analysis, Americans have built a more egalitarian society, with more entrepreneurship and individual geographic and economic mobility, than are found in Europe. Has something like the same thing been true of the nation's relations with other countries? As it has unfolded over the past two-and-one-half centuries, that is, has American foreign policy displayed an exceptional character as well?

One answer to that question, an answer popular among many professional students of international relations, is that it has not. From this perspective, all countries conduct their foreign policies in similar ways because all find themselves in the same situation. They all must live in an international system that is "anarchic"—without a supreme authority to keep order—which means that each must protect itself from all the others. In these circumstances, it follows, every sovereign state must attend to its own power, above all its military power, and maneuver so as to maximize its chances of survival, and sometimes, when survival is assured, its opportunities for expansion.

This school of thought about international affairs bears the name "realism" in American academic discourse because it posits that independent countries always and everywhere conduct themselves in conformity with the harsh realities of the international system. Since all sovereign states, including the strongest of them, have had to take this fundamental feature of international politics into account for centuries, other languages have terms to denote it. The relevant German word is *Realpolitik*. The comparable French phrase is *raison d'etat*. A synonym in English is "power politics." All refer to the tendency, which goes back to the Greek city-states of the fifth century B.C.E. as described in the account of the Peloponnesian Wars by Thucydides, of independent political communities to act to defend themselves and their interests by the threat or the actual use of force.

Foreign-policy realism resembles the neoclassical study of economics, which proceeds from the assumption that individuals and firms also exhibit a fundamental similarity: all seek to maximize their "utility"—that is, their well-being. The analogy can be extended to human beings, who have basic genetic, physiological, and anatomical features in common. In fundamental ways, all members of the species *Homo sapiens* are alike, a fact that makes the art and science of medicine possible.

All human beings are not, of course, alike in every way, and certainly not in every important way. They go about their lives differently, and they do so because their personalities differ—personality being the collection of character traits and behavioral inclinations that an individual acquires at an early age and that persist, while sometimes undergoing modifications, throughout his or her lifetime. So it is, as well, with sovereign states in their relations with others. Their conduct also varies according to their differing sizes and geographical circumstances as well as their particular histories, political values, social structures, and public institutions. To be sure, each state must see to its own survival in the anarchic international order; but the way they all seek to survive, and what they do and attempt to do beyond surviving, has depended on the widely varying features of their political personalities.

The United States has its own political personality, three particular recurring features of which have made its foreign policy different from the foreign policies of other countries. These three distinctively American features, that is, have made American foreign policy, like American society and politics, exceptional. The first of them concerns the goals of the nation's foreign policy beyond survival. Such goals have emerged, to an unusually great extent, from the dominant political ideas of the United States. The second enduring feature of American foreign policy involves the means by which the American government has sought to achieve its various goals: more than other countries, it has attempted to use economic instruments to secure political ends. The third and final element of American foreign-policy exceptionalism is the way the country has, over the course of its history, decided and carried out its foreign policies. The American public, both as a whole and through organized groups, has had more influence over what the United States has done abroad than has been the case in other countries.

American foreign policy qualifies as exceptional not only because of the relative prominence, in its formulation and execution, of political ideas, economic levers, and public influence, but also because those three features are in some sense the opposites of what has historically been the norm in the rest of the world. Most countries, most of the time, have conducted broadly realist foreign policies, without much regard to whatever their dominant political ideas happened to be. Most countries, most of the time, have used political instruments to secure economic goals rather than, as often in the American case, the reverse. And in most countries, most of the time, a small circle of officials has dominated relations with other sovereign states and has paid relatively little attention to what the people of the country have thought or wanted. In foreign policy, the United States counts, therefore, as an international outlier. The history of its relations with the rest of the world displays a distinctively American way of foreign policy.

***

Most of the political ideas, institutions, and practices that the United States has aspired to spread beyond its borders since the eighteenth century have to do with liberty in one form or another and may be grouped together under the heading "liberal." These ideas pertain to the treatment of individuals within countries, to the composition and governance of states, and to conditions in the international system as a whole. How the United States has promoted its liberal political ideas internationally over the decades is the subject of Chapter 1 of this book.

The most venerable American political idea makes liberty the country's supreme political value. It holds that individuals have rights—another term for liberty in the American lexicon—upon which the government may not encroach. States that operate according to democratic principles are likely to respect the rights of their citizens, and for that reason the United States has sought to foster, and sometimes even to install, democratic governments beyond North America. Americans have believed, especially since the early years of the twentieth century, that sovereign states composed of single nations—that is, nation-states—are more likely than other political communities to practice democracy. The United States has consequently endorsed and encouraged national self-determination as the basis for sovereignty. As for the international system as a whole, America has championed arrangements and practices designed to create and sustain peace among its members. Finally, a belief in the possibility, sometimes even the inevitability, of human progress has undergirded the various American foreign policies intended, from the eighteenth century to the twenty-first, to promote individual rights, national self-determination, and peace. The nation's foreign policy, like other aspects of American life, has proceeded on the assumption, which emerged from the Enlightenment—a series of political, philosophical, and scientific developments in eighteenth-century Europe—that political conditions everywhere can, should, and will be changed for the better.

When the thirteen colonies declared their independence, these liberal ideas did not inform the institutions and practices of other countries. To the contrary, most eighteenth-century states had autocratic governments that assumed no obligation to respect the individual rights that were so important to Americans. Empires, not nation-states, dominated the planet, and empires typically included several, sometimes many, different national groups. Usually, one of the nations controlled the others; and the others typically had joined the empire involuntarily, by virtue of having been conquered. Finally, most states at the time concerned themselves with preparing for, fighting, and winning armed conflicts and gave little or no attention to fostering international conditions in which such conflicts would not take place. When it first appeared, therefore, the American foreign policy of promoting liberal ideas sought to create in the world what the Latin motto on the great seal of the United States proclaimed that the new nation represented in North America: a *novus ordo seclorum*—a new order of the ages.

The distinctively idea-driven American foreign policy is sometimes called "idealism," to distinguish it from realism. Another term for it is "ideological." The word is appropriate in this context because it refers to a belief system oriented to action,[2] which accurately describes American foreign-policy liberalism. While the American ideology is not laid out in canonical texts—in contrast, for example, to Marxism–Leninism— it has had a comparable impact on the United States. It has had, in fact, more influence in the world than Marxism, which became a hollow creed when it ceased to command serious belief in the Soviet Union, the country with political and economic systems based on its precepts. By contrast, from the founding of the republic, Americans genuinely and often fervently believed in their own political ideas, and still do.

The term "ideology" can have negative connotations by virtue of its association with the totalitarian powers that the United States opposed during the twentieth century. Nazi Germany and the Soviet Union sought to impose their political ideas on other countries by force. The United States has used force to promote international liberalism infrequently and usually defensively, most often to protect liberal institutions and practices against illiberal assaults on them. America has not, on the whole—albeit with some exceptions—tried to impose its political ideas and institutions forcibly on others.

Moreover, the *content* of the American foreign-policy ideology, with its emphasis on liberty, differs fundamentally from fascism's and communism's subjugation of individuals to all-powerful governments that they cannot affect, let alone peacefully remove. It is hardly accidental that much of the world has embraced liberalism while rejecting and resisting the ideologies of the totalitarians. The ideas of American foreign policy, different from the ideologies of fascism and communism in almost every significant respect, do, however, have one feature in common with them: the United States, too, has aspired to spread its ideas beyond its borders. Americans generally think of themselves as having principles rather than an ideology; but for the purposes of this book that is a distinction without a difference.

Relatively few sovereign states have conducted ideological foreign policies, and fewer still have invested as much effort as the United States has for this purpose; but every country has had policies governing its economic relations with the rest of the world. In most cases, these policies, like the economic activities of individuals everywhere, have aimed at maximizing economic well-being. To this end, sovereign states have frequently employed the political tools available to them, chiefly diplomacy and the threat and/or the use of force, to enhance their well-being. Such, for example, was a fundamental reason, for most of history, for establishing and maintaining empires. Although not unknown, the reverse of this widespread pattern—that is, the use of economic tools (trade and finance)—to secure political goals has occurred less frequently; but it has appeared more often in American history than in the histories of other countries. Chapter 2 of *The American Way of Foreign Policy* concerns the country's deployment, from the eighteenth century to the twenty-first, of economic instruments in pursuit of political aims.

As for America's foreign policymaking process, in the eighteenth century, democratic governments were rare. Almost no political system then afforded opportunities for the public to exert influence on policies of any kind, including foreign policy. In the two-and-one-half centuries since the birth of the American republic, many more governments have come to be accountable to the people they govern. Still, the United States has remained exceptional for the range of opportunities afforded both non-governmental groups and the public as a whole to affect America's relations with other countries. How they have made use of those opportunities is the subject of Chapter 3 of this book.

To summarize: the United States has conducted an exceptional foreign policy in that its policy has consistently been, in comparison with the foreign policies of other countries, unusually ideological, unusually economic, and unusually democratic. To that assertion, however, three qualifications must be added.

First, the United States is not the only country ever to have conducted foreign policies of this kind. In the nineteenth century, for example, even while presiding over a large empire that did not offer self-determination to its subject peoples, Great Britain occasionally sought to foster liberal ideas and practices beyond its borders. In the 1870s, to cite one instance, it objected vociferously to the oppression of the Bulgarians by their Ottoman Turkish overlords.[3] This was an early campaign, although not a conspicuously successful one, on behalf of human rights. To cite another example, since 1945, the countries of Western Europe, acting jointly during the various stages of economic and political integration among them that produced the European Union, have staunchly advocated the liberal ideas and values that the United States has propounded since the eighteenth century.

In the use of economic instruments for political purposes, in the twentieth and twenty-first centuries, other countries have joined the United States in imposing economic sanctions in response to policies of which they disapprove, in the hope of compelling the offending country to change the policy in question. As for the third distinct feature of American foreign policy, as democracy has taken firm hold in Western Europe and spread around the world since 1945, more and more countries have devised their foreign policies not only through the decisions of the political elite but also, to some degree at least, in response to the wishes of the public at large. The foreign policy of the United States qualifies as exceptional, in short, not because other countries have never exhibited its distinguishing features but rather because these features have appeared over a longer period of time, more frequently, and have had greater weight, in America than elsewhere.

Moreover, and this is the second qualification, American foreign policy has not proceeded in an entirely exceptional way. The United States has itself conducted foreign policies of the kind that have been historically normal for other countries. "Realist" considerations of power and security have scarcely been absent from America's relations with the rest of the world. It has waged wars and, since the middle of the twentieth century, maintained a large military establishment in peacetime. Indeed, when having to choose between a realist policy of defending its interests and an ideological effort to spread its ideas and values, the American government has more often than not opted for the defense of interests.[4] Perhaps the best-known, but hardly the only, example is the alliance that the United States made in World War II with the totalitarian Soviet Union against the similarly illiberal and murderous, but more directly threatening to American interests, Nazi Germany. The two American presidents most committed to fostering American political ideas around the world, and above all doing away with the ancient institution of war—Thomas Jefferson and Woodrow Wilson[5]—themselves presided over American military operations abroad.

As well as employing economic means in pursuit of political ends, the United States has also, like other countries, reversed the order, making use of political instruments of policy for the purpose of achieving economic goals. American policy in East Asia during the second half of the nineteenth century—opening Japan and Korea to trade and announcing an "Open Door" policy for China as a tactic to preserve American economic access to that country—involved military and diplomatic initiatives in the service of American economic interests.[6] More recently, the United States assumed the political and military responsibility for assuring the free flow of oil from the Persian Gulf, on which the smooth functioning of the global economy has depended.

Finally, the American government on occasion has wielded the kind of authority over relations with other countries, at the expense of the popular influence, that countries governed autocratically routinely practice. During the Cold War, the executive branch ordered military forces into action without explicit congressional approval often enough to give rise to the idea that the United States had encumbered itself with an "imperial presidency."[7]

The third qualification that the "exceptionalist" thesis of *The American Way of Foreign Policy* requires is that, in the United States as elsewhere, foreign policies have routinely had more than a single purpose. National motives, like human ones, tend to be mixed. Thus, even when America has acted to promote its political ideas, it has also frequently and sometimes simultaneously sought to protect and enhance its security. It took part in the three great global conflicts of the twentieth century—the two world wars and the Cold War—in order to protect democracy and national self-determination but also to counteract the military power of aggressive countries that threatened not only these political practices but also the security of the United States. In each case, that is, America waged both an ideological and a realist war.

Similarly, the large-scale transfer of capital from the United States to Western Europe in the years immediately after World War II had both political and economic goals. American financial generosity aspired to revive the war-battered economies of the Continent for the purposes both of staving off communist subversion and enriching the Western Europeans and ultimately Americans as well—and succeeded on both counts. Likewise, American foreign policies have not always originated entirely in the councils of the government or wholly in response to the wishes of American society as a whole. Often both were at work simultaneously.

Historical events, including the events that comprise the history of American foreign policy, do not divide neatly into binary categories such as ideological or realist motives, political or economic goals, top-down or bottom-up initiatives. History is the realm of both/and, not either/or.* What makes American foreign policy exceptional is the

---

* As the historian Charles S. Maier has put it, "History remains an overdetermined system of developments, so there will always be scope for argumentation and persuasive narratives on both sides." Charles S. Maier, *Among Empires: American Ascendancy and Its Predecessors*, Cambridge, Massachusetts: Harvard University Press, 2006, p. 124. It might be added that differing narratives of particular historical events and trends might both (or all) have a measure of validity.

frequency and the prominence, in comparison with the foreign policies of other countries, of ideological aims, the use of economic instruments in pursuit of political goals, and the influence of the public on devising and carrying out policies toward other countries.

***

Each of the three enduring features of American foreign policy appeared even before the United States achieved sovereign independence, but the first two—ideology and economics—became increasingly prominent over the course of the next 250 years. That occurred because, over that span of time, the United States became increasingly powerful and, power being the currency of international relations, the more power a country has, the greater its potential becomes for exerting influence on others. From the eighteenth century to the twenty-first, America's potential expanded dramatically. Beginning as a loosely connected collection of British colonies strung out along the east coast of North America, it became, successively, an independent country that was weak in comparison with the great powers of Europe, then one of several great powers in the international system, next one of two nuclear-armed superpowers with global reach, and finally, in the quarter-century following 1990, the world's only hyperpower, towering above all countries, without major challengers to its primacy.[8]

As the United States grew more powerful, the opportunities to make the world more liberal increased, yielding more, more active, and more ambitious American initiatives for this purpose. At the same time, the American economy expanded rapidly, ultimately becoming the largest in the world. This provided more and more economic resources with which to pursue political goals.

The increase in American power led to more frequent and more ambitious ideological and economic foreign policies. Thus, Chapter 1 and Chapter 2, which deal with those policies, are organized, after an introductory overview in the first section, chronologically. By contrast, from the country's beginning, the American public had a major say in national policy of all kinds, including foreign policy. So Chapter 3, on the domestic character of American foreign policymaking, is organized differently—according to the major ways in which American society has shaped American foreign policy since the eighteenth century.

The accounts of the ideological, economic, and democratic features of that foreign policy across four different centuries inevitably raise a question: what impact have these three enduring features had on the history of the United States and the rest of the world? The Conclusion to *The American Way of Foreign Policy* addresses that question.

An Ideological Foreign Policy

IDEOLOGY AND FOREIGN POLICY

For almost all of history, the foreign policies of most countries have revolved around power, above all military power, and the uses to which they have put it: the defense of their own territory and the conquest of the territory of others. Military power has certainly played a large role in the foreign policy of the United States. America has fought twelve significant wars* since its founding and engaged in many other lesser military conflicts. In the eighteenth century, it secured independence from the British Empire. In the first half of the nineteenth, it expanded its borders to encompass all of North America between Canada and Mexico, often through the threat of war and sometimes through war itself. In the second half of the twentieth century and through the first quarter of the twenty-first, it fielded the most powerful and expansive armed forces on the planet. What the realist approach deems central to the theory and practice of foreign policy has been abundantly present in America's relations with the rest of the world.

Yet American foreign policy, from the beginning, has had another component that has set it apart from the foreign policies of other countries. Beyond their borders, Americans, more than other peoples, have sought to propagate their own political ideas. In addition to the pursuit of power politics—at times reinforcing that pursuit and at other

---

* They are the Revolutionary War, the War of 1812, the Mexican War, the Civil War, the Spanish–American War, World War I, World War II, the Korean War, the Vietnam War, the Gulf War, the War in Afghanistan, and the War in Iraq.

times conflicting with it—the United States has conducted an ideological foreign policy.

In the constellation of political values that Americans and their government have sought to disseminate, liberty has held pride of place. The Declaration of Independence of 1776, the country's founding document, places liberty second only to life itself on the list of rights to which all people are entitled. The word adorns American coins. Benjamin Franklin observed in Americans "a special enthusiasm for liberty"[1] and Abraham Lincoln called liberty "the first precept of our ancient faith."[2]

Liberty comes in three varieties: political liberty, which is enshrined in the first ten amendments to the American Constitution of 1787, which are known collectively as the Bill of Rights (rights are sometimes used as a synonym for liberties); religious liberty, which dates back to the colonial era; and economic liberty, above all the right to private property, which the colonies inherited from their English progenitor. In the second half of the twentieth century, the United States added to the array of liberties it worked to defend and spread what came to be called human rights, meaning the right of individuals to be safe from lethal predations by their own governments.

The political ideas that the United States has sought to encourage and sometimes directly to implement abroad affect not only individuals but also the political collectives in which individuals live—sovereign states. Americans have strongly preferred that states be composed according to the national principle. Sovereignty, they have believed, should rest with national groups rather than, as was the global norm in the eighteenth and nineteenth centuries, multinational empires. From the beginning, the United States made itself an opponent of empires, including the one from which it wrested its independence.

America had, as well, a clear preference for the way nation-states ought to be governed: democratically. The democracy that the United States favored, and that many countries adopted beginning in the second half of the twentieth century, combines two distinct political traditions. One is popular sovereignty, from which this form of government—rule by the people (in Greek, the *demos*)—takes its name. The second basic ingredient of twentieth- and twenty-first-century democracy is liberty.

For much of history, liberty—which, by defining protected areas for individuals, imposes limits on what governments may do—was widely regarded as not only distinct from, but also actually incompatible with, popular sovereignty, which defines how governments are chosen. In the twentieth century, however, the two traditions fused into a single form of political organization,[3] and American support for the combination of the two around the world became central to its ideological approach to foreign policy.

The United States has not only advocated democracy, it has also occasionally attempted to install it directly. At the end of the twentieth century, this project, which in fact began in the nineteenth century, acquired the name "nation-building." That term, although widely used, is misleading, indeed inaccurate. Nations are groups of people who believe that they have a common destiny (and therefore, in most cases, deserve their own state) by virtue of a common language, or religion, or ethnicity, or history. Nationalism is therefore, at root, a psychological and emotional property and cannot be put in place by any outside party. In the episodes of its foreign policy commonly called nation-building, the United States sought to build the organs of governance: parliaments, executives, legal systems, judiciaries, armed forces, and the like. It was seeking, that is, to design and install the institutions that comprise a state. It was thus engaged in state-building,[4] which is another recurrent feature of the ideological component of American foreign policy.

In addition to individuals and states, American foreign policy has addressed the society of states—the international system. In particular, it has aspired to put an end to a continuing feature of that system, whose prominence in international history gave rise to the realist approach to foreign policy—namely, war. On occasion, the world has enjoyed a respite from war through a balance of power between and among its most formidable states, and in its 250 years of existence, the United States has sometimes sought to foster, and even itself taken part in, a stable balance of power.

More than other countries, however, and while hardly a pacifist country and sometimes not even an especially peaceful one, America has hoped for, and tried to provide, a more solid and enduring basis for non-belligerency. Peace, defined not simply as the temporary absence of armed conflict but rather as a permanent condition of international affairs,[5] counts, along with individual liberty and democracy, as one of the three political ideas that the United States has tried to put into practice beyond its own borders.

In pursuit of peace of this kind, the American government has over the years employed several techniques, with only intermittent and modest but not entirely negligible success. It has attempted to eliminate, or at least to limit, armaments, on the assumption, shared by many Americans over the years, that abolishing the instruments of warfare would put an end to war itself.[6] While technically true, that proposition rests on a mistake about causality in international relations. States do not become adversaries because they arm themselves. Rather, they arm themselves because they must deal with adversaries; and their adversarial relationships have their roots both in the structure of the international system and in conflicting political goals. Politics, not weaponry, causes wars; and politics, with the hopes, fears, preferences, and aversions that it entails, is not susceptible to abolition. Still, the United States has periodically managed to arrange internationally agreed-upon limits on armaments; and these limits, which themselves arise from political calculations rather than the expectation of doing away with war forever, have for a time made the world at least modestly more peaceful than it was without them.

The American government has also on occasion sought to mediate between and among hostile, sometimes warring countries; and mediation, where successful, has reduced international conflict. In addition, on two occasions—after the two world wars of the first half of the twentieth century—the United States has taken the lead in establishing an international organization designed to keep the peace. Neither the League of Nations nor the United Nations (UN), however, managed to fulfill the hopes of their founders by terminating international conflict.

The United States has also championed international law as a vehicle for peace, although neither it nor any other country has ever found a way to establish a mechanism for enforcing that law, as governments do within sovereign states. The most ambitious proponents of the

League of Nations and the UN, among them Americans and in the first case an American president, Woodrow Wilson, saw those two organizations as, potentially, the functional equivalents of a world government. To fulfill that potential, however, existing states, including the United States, would have had to have surrendered major sovereign prerogatives to these organizations. This the countries of the world—including the United States—proved unwilling to do. Still, the violation of two particular international laws—against transgressing the rights of neutral countries in wartime and against cross-border aggression—have had a significant impact on American foreign policy, contributing materially to American decisions to go to war.

Finally, underlying all of America's efforts to bring the rest of the world into conformity with American political ideas has been the confidence, inherited ultimately from the European Enlightenment, that human beings can improve their individual and collective conditions.[7] From the beginning, America's ideological foreign policy has rested on a belief in the possibility of progress and the conviction that the United States could and should act as the agent of that progress. Thomas Paine, a celebrated troubadour of American independence, in words that would resonate with succeeding generations, wrote that "We have it in our power to begin the world over again."[8]

Individual liberty, national self-determination, democracy, and peace: these are the major ideas for which Americans have sought to make their foreign policy the vehicle since the founding of the republic. The term often applied to the program they collectively constitute is "liberal," and that term is broadly accurate. Its root is, after all, liberty. Self-determination applies to entire nations the liberty of individuals—freedom from arbitrary, oppressive, uncontrolled authority. Democracy has as one of its two constituent parts liberty. Peace, as America has often envisioned it, qualifies as liberal in the sense that it comes about not as an equilibrium achieved through the military strength of various countries, but rather by voluntary agreement between and among them of the kind practiced in the domestic politics of liberal democracies.

Why have these political ideas had unusual prominence in the history of American foreign policy? The pattern dates from the beginning of the republic. The memory of the establishment of the United States as an independent country has always loomed large in American public life, as origin stories tend to do in the lives of political communities. In their own eyes, the Americans made their revolution, as they came to call it, above all on behalf of liberty. They considered the taxes the British government was attempting to impose without their consent to be a plot to deprive the colonies of the liberty they had always enjoyed—they in fact had largely governed themselves[9]—and were entitled always to enjoy. Thomas Jefferson said at the time that the defense of liberty was "the whole object of the present controversy."[10] George Washington described his mission as "the maintenance and preservation of American liberties."[11] More than any other consideration, it was this central political idea, and the need to defend it, that impelled the thirteen colonies to leave the British Empire and create their own political community.[12] The defense and promotion of liberty and other related ideas have pervaded American public life ever since.

In the nation's history after the Revolution, moreover, American political ideas not only retained their importance for the United States, they also expanded it as a result of America's singular character. Most countries consist of people who share major cultural characteristics—language, religion, and ethnicity being the most salient—and whose ancestors have lived on the same territory for generations. This is not the case for the United States: its inhabitants or their forebears came from elsewhere—first from northern, then southern and eastern Europe as well as (involuntarily) from Africa, then from Asia and Latin America.

For that reason, American national identity, and the sense of community that underlies it, could not have roots in "blood and soil," as was the case for the English, the French, the Italians, and others. What Americans, with their diverse backgrounds, had in common was an allegiance to a set of ideas—the liberal ideas that the United States has attempted to implement at home and to disseminate abroad.[13] Some immigrants made their way to North America expressly for the purpose of living in a country where liberty reigned. More immigrated in search of economic opportunity, but most of them came to understand that embracing these dominant political ideas of their adopted homeland was an integral part of their new nationality.[14]

Yet another reason for the prominence of ideas in the domestic and international affairs of the United States is the major role that religion has played in its national life, from the colonial period onward,[15] despite the absence of a European-style established church. Notably, the religious tradition that shaped America was the Protestantism derived from the northern European Reformation of the sixteenth century, and in particular its English and Scottish offshoots. It was Protestants who first settled North America from the British Isles. The Protestant version of Christianity is compatible, in ways that other versions are not (or at least were not), with the political ideas the Americans adopted. Not surprisingly, religious concepts seeped into political activities.[†] In *Democracy in America*, his well-known assessment of the United States in the early 1830s, the Frenchman Alexis de Tocqueville wrote that "[t]he Americans combine the notions of Christianity and of liberty so intimately in their minds that it is impossible to make them conceive of one without the other."[16] Indeed, the dominant American political ideas have functioned as the secular counterparts of the dominant American religious tradition. That tradition emphasizes the individual's personal relationship with the Almighty, unmediated by a hierarchical religious establishment, such as the Vatican is to the Catholic church.[17] Protestantism and the American political creed both have the individual—the believer in the first case, the citizen in the second—at their core.

North American Protestantism, in its several denominations, particularly encouraged an ideological foreign policy because of its strong evangelical bent.[18] American Protestants have felt a calling to spread their faith within the United States, leading to waves of evangelical fervor known as "Great Awakenings"—religious revivals that took place

---

[†] James Kurth, *The American Way of Empire*, Washington, DC: Washington Books, 2019, p. 77. The mixture of the religious and the political continued into the twenty-first century. President George W. Bush "often spoke of freedom as God's gift to America and to mankind and of America's calling to be the light of the world and bring freedom to everyone." *Ibid.*, pp. 77–78.

periodically between the eighteenth and twentieth centuries. Beginning at the end of the nineteenth century, the calling also encompassed bringing the word of God to peoples beyond North America through missionary work. It was natural, given the power of this tradition, for a sense of mission to become part of American foreign policy as well.

In addition, at the end of the nineteenth century, American Protestants came to believe in salvation not only through faith but also through good works.[19] This "Social Gospel" movement helped to inspire the Progressive Movement of the early twentieth century, with its array of reforms aimed at purging corruption from government. In foreign policy, the Social Gospel encouraged the various efforts at international improvement that the American government undertook in the twentieth and twenty-first centuries.

Finally, the United States has conducted an unusually ideological foreign policy because it has had the luxury of doing so. Considerations of power politics crowd out ideology in the foreign policies of countries that face imminent threats and must therefore concentrate on defending themselves against these threats however they can. For the weak and the beleaguered, power trumps ideas. Unusually among sovereign states, for most of its history America did not face urgent threats to its political independence and thus enjoyed the freedom to make the propagation of its own political ideas a major part of its relations with other countries.

This was not entirely the case in the fifty years from 1765, when the Revolution began as a protest against a British tax known as the Stamp Act, to 1815, when the Napoleonic Wars, into which the recently established United States had been involuntarily drawn, came to an end. In this period, America waged two wars against Great Britain—the second being the War of 1812, which ended in 1815. Even in those conflicts, however, the British, while fielding superior military forces and inflicting major battlefield defeats on the Americans, could not hope to conquer and occupy the towns and cities along the eastern coast of North America where most Americans lived, let alone the seemingly endless interior that the Americans were in the process of settling. By 1838, Abraham Lincoln could say that

All the armies of Europe, Asia and Africa combined, with all the treasure of the earth (our own excepted) in their military chest; with a Buonaparte for a commander, could not by force take a drink from the Ohio, or make a track on the Blue Ridge, in a trial of a thousand years.[20]

In the hundred years between 1815 and 1915, Great Britain's Royal Navy patrolled the Atlantic Ocean, making it impossible for any of Europe's other great powers to molest the United States; and Britain itself was able to secure its interests in the Western Hemisphere without a third war with its former colonies. After 1915, the United States did become ever more deeply engaged with other countries, but by then it operated from a position of strength, free of the fear of conquest with which lesser powers have had to cope and thus able to devote itself, in part, to fostering liberty, democracy, and peace beyond its borders.

To summarize: the origins and the national identity of the United States gave its political ideas an unusual importance; the early, continuing, and pervasive influence of Protestant Christianity both reinforced their importance and helped to foster a disposition to spread them beyond North America; and the country's exceptional freedom from the imminent threat of conquest afforded it the opportunity to conduct a foreign policy designed not only to protect the American homeland but also to try to make the world over in the American image.

1783–1914

The American Revolution was an ideological event, motivated by a set of political ideas that, in the decades thereafter, embedded themselves in the public life of the independent country that the Revolution produced. Initially however, the United States did little to try to spread those ideas beyond North America. It did not conduct an aggressively ideological foreign policy except, occasionally, rhetorically.

This foreign policy of restraint, of non-intervention, of concentrating its national energies on North America, is sometimes known as "isolationism."[21] Insofar as the term implies a lack of engagement of any kind with other countries, or a lack of interest in the world beyond America's borders, it is seriously misleading. From the first, the United States sought trade with the world on as wide a scale as it could. Moreover, the country was scarcely indifferent to the fate of liberty, democracy, and peace beyond its borders. When other peoples took steps to put liberal political ideas into practice, Americans approved; and the American government publicly expressed that approval.[22]

Americans welcomed, for example, the success of the Latin American republics in freeing themselves from Spanish imperial rule in the early nineteenth century, although the government in Washington delayed according them official recognition until after the United States had completed a treaty with Spain that ceded territory in North America to the United States.[23] Americans also applauded the Greek revolt against the Ottoman Empire in 1822 and the anti-monarchical uprisings that erupted across Europe in 1848.[24] The United States subsequently welcomed and honored one of the leaders of the 1848 uprising in Hungary, Lajos Kossuth.[25] Toward the end of the century, in an early episode of human rights advocacy, the American government protested the assaults on Jews living in the Russian Empire.[26]

If the United States did nothing concrete to support its own principles in these instances, this was because it lacked the capacity to offer anything stronger than supportive words. It did not have the military might to intervene, or even to threaten to intervene, much less to provide serious military assistance, far beyond its borders. Nor, despite a commitment to the use of economic instruments to achieve political goals,[27] could it exert significant economic pressure abroad. America was, in short, insufficiently powerful to take effective active steps to spread its political ideas.

This did not mean, however, that the new republic forswore international influence. To the contrary, it hoped, indeed expected, that other countries would adopt American political ideas, institutions, and practices through the power of the American example. The United States would change the world, its citizens believed in the nineteenth century and indeed thereafter, simply by existing. Its existence, and the success of its political system in protecting and promoting life, liberty, and human happiness, would inspire the other people and their governments to emulate America. Leaving the presidency in 1809, Thomas Jefferson called the United States "the only monument of human rights, the sole depository of the sacred fire of freedom and self-government, from hence it is to be lighted up in other regions of the earth."[28]

The idea of American exemplarism has a long history. In 1630, the Puritan leader John Winthrop, preaching on the ship *Arbella* that was carrying him and his fellow believers to the New World, foresaw that the Massachusetts Bay Colony they were founding would "be as a city up on a hill. The eyes of all people are upon us."[29] He did not suggest that the city's inhabitants would descend from the hill and go out into the world to reform it according to their lights; but in the twentieth century, that is what the people of the country to which Massachusetts and other colonies gave rise began to do.

In the wake of securing its independence, and for a hundred years thereafter, the United States largely refrained from foreign military interventions.[‡] While its weakness was one reason for this restraint, and an important one, there was another: the often-expressed fear that war, and the creation of armed forces to wage it, would subvert the very liberty the colonials had risked, as their Declaration of Independence put it, "our lives, our fortunes, and our sacred honor" to achieve. Rather than expanding liberty abroad, Americans feared, a forceful, aggressive foreign policy would instead extinguish it at home.

Historical examples, from the Roman republic's transformation into an autocracy to Napoleon's seizure of power in France at the end of the eighteenth century, had taught this lesson,[30] and Americans absorbed it. "The fetters imposed on liberty at home," the future president James Madison said, "have ever been forged out of the weapons provided for defense against real, pretended, or imaginary dangers from abroad."[31] President Woodrow Wilson initially resisted American involvement in

---

[‡] The Mexican War of 1846 to 1848 was the conspicuous exception but was in keeping with the major theme of American history of that era. The United States went to war against Mexico as part of its great national project of the first half of the nineteenth century of expanding its territory to reach the Pacific Ocean.

the European war that began in 1914 because, he said, "war means autocracy."[32] In 1938, anticipating American participation in another such conflict, the antiwar senator Gerald Nye, a North Dakota Republican, said that "the one sure way to kill off democracy in the United States is to enter another war."[33]

The fear they all expressed was not entirely groundless. A recurrent pattern in American history illustrates the threat that war can pose to freedom: dangers to the republic, perceived and real, led to measures that restricted liberty, measures the public largely supported or at least accepted.

The ongoing conflict with Great Britain and France over America's neutral shipping rights during the Wars of the French Revolution created a climate of opinion in which the Congress approved the Alien and Sedition Acts in 1798. These laws permitted the arrest, imprisonment, and deportation of non-citizens during wartime and placed limits, contrary to the First Amendment to the Constitution, on political speech and publications.[34]

During the Civil War, Abraham Lincoln, a man who did as much for liberty as any individual in American history or indeed the history of any country, concluded that the security of the Union he was waging a bloody war to preserve required the suspension of the ancient English right, which the United States had inherited, of habeas corpus—the legal procedure that prohibits the government from holding an individual in custody indefinitely without showing just cause for doing so.[35]

In the Second World War, suspicions—which proved unfounded—that Americans of Japanese descent would work secretly on behalf of America's adversary Japan caused President Franklin D. Roosevelt to approve the removal of 117,000 Japanese Americans from the West Coast communities in which they lived to internment camps in the country's interior, in gross violation of their rights.[36]

The early years of the Cold War and the Korean War gave rise to a national search, whose most aggressive participant was Senator Joseph McCarthy of Wisconsin, for communists and their active sympathizers in the United States.[37] The Soviet Union was indeed conducting espionage in the United States, but what came to be called McCarthyism affected several thousand Americans who were not spies, costing them their livelihoods.[38] They were penalized for political views that some of them had long abandoned or indeed had never held. In less fraught times, such views might have carried a social and political stigma, but, because of the constitutional guarantee of political liberty, would not have placed those who held them in legal jeopardy.

Finally, the terrorist attacks of September 11, 2001, led to policies that impinged on Americans' liberties by authorizing the collection by the government of "meta-data"—that is, the identities of the senders and recipients of telephone calls and emails deemed suspicious, although not the content of those messages. Non-Americans suffered harsher consequences. Some suspected of terrorism were sent to prisons outside the United States, where the protections to which prisoners in the United States are entitled did not apply.[39]

None of these violations of the country's supreme political value, however, confirmed the worst fears about the impact of war on the American republic. The setbacks for liberty invariably proved temporary. Once the sense of national peril had passed, the illiberal measures were largely withdrawn, or modified, or ignored. Whatever else may be said about America's wars, they have not transformed the country from a democracy into an autocracy.

The most important event in American history in the hundred years between 1815 to 1915 was the Civil War, which was fought from 1861 to 1865. It had only a modest foreign-policy dimension.[40] It did, however, involve the ideas that have pervaded America's domestic and foreign policies. In that sense it qualifies as an ideological war. One of the aims of the Union side in the war was the abolition of slavery, the most illiberal and, given the centrality of liberty in the nation's pantheon of political ideas, arguably the most un-American institution in the history of the United States.

The elimination of slavery only became a goal of the North a year and a half after the conflict had begun. From its start, President Abraham Lincoln made it clear that he was seeking, first and foremost, to save the Union. Saving the Union, he believed, would have profound international consequences. If it were not saved, not only Americans but also people everywhere would suffer a major political loss. For in that case the example of representative government that the United States offered the world would be discredited; and the chances for that form of government to flourish elsewhere depended on the continuing force of the American example.[41] That is why Lincoln concluded his address at the battlefield at Gettysburg, Pennsylvania, on November 19, 1863—the best-known public speech in American history—with the plea to continue the "unfinished work" of the war so that "government of the people, by the people, for the people shall not perish from the earth." In the eyes of the commander-in-chief, the Civil War was being waged not only to end slavery but also to sustain American exemplarism.

The aftermath of the war introduced another feature of America's ideological approach to foreign policy, although in this case within the borders of the United States. The period of Reconstruction in the former Confederacy may be understood as an exercise in state-building.[42] The federal government attempted to install a new political system in the South in which former slaves would enjoy political liberty and economic opportunity. The project did not succeed. It fell victim to the problems that state-building beyond North America would encounter in the twentieth and twenty-first centuries. To take root and endure, a new political order must be accepted by the people who are part of it; and for this to happen, the new order must be compatible with the local values, beliefs, and experiences—that is, with the local political culture. A political system based on the equality of all people did not accord with the political culture of the Southern whites, who did not accept it. Instead, they actively resisted it. For a time, the national government enforced it with federal troops but then grew weary of doing so and withdrew them. With the mechanism for enforcing it gone, whites in the South succeeded in overturning much of the new order.[43] That pattern would repeat itself at other times in other places.

In 1898, with the Spanish–American War, the period in which the United States conducted an ideological foreign policy strictly by example came to an end, and the era of more active efforts to spread American political ideas around the world began. That war unfolded in two stages. First, the United States invaded Cuba, an island in the

Caribbean ninety miles from the coast of the North American mainland, to put an end to Spanish mistreatment of the inhabitants of what was at the time a Spanish colony. In the second, the American naval squadron in the Pacific attacked and defeated the Spanish fleet based in another Spanish imperial possession, the Philippine archipelago. After the military victory, the American government decided to annex the Philippines. This triggered an insurrection that took more than three years for American troops to suppress.

The Spanish–American War furnished the occasion for the pursuit of two ideological goals. The United States went to Cuba to rescue the Cubans from the Spanish, in what became America's first episode of humanitarian intervention.[44] Having periodically deplored government assaults on the people they governed during the nineteenth century, at that century's end the United States had become powerful enough to use military means to put an end to such an assault in a neighboring country. Then, having assumed responsibility for governing the Philippines, the American government undertook to implant modern institutions of governance there, making it the first instance of American state-building outside the continental United States.[45]

The state-building took place in what had become, by virtue of the annexation, an American possession. As a result of the Spanish–American War, the United States acquired what the great powers of Europe had long had: an empire. This seemed, both at the time and in retrospect, anomalous—indeed, hypocritical or worse. For America had always opposed empires. It had created itself as an act of rebellion against the British Empire. It had consistently favored national self-determination, the antithesis of imperial rule.[46] The subjects of empires did not enjoy the self-government that Abraham Lincoln and earlier leaders of the United States had identified as their nation's gift to the world. Empire deprived people of what Americans valued most highly—political liberty. All this raises a question: just how sharply did the events of 1898 and their consequences depart from the American way of foreign policy?

The question is not a simple one to answer because the word "empire" has come to be applied to various forms of international inequality.[47] In the nineteenth century, the meaning was straightforward: it denoted rule over foreigners,[48] with the use of force central to the enterprise. Imperial powers acquired their empires by conquest, and while almost all imperial rule involved some measure of cooperation between the imperial masters and at least some of their subjects, the rulers ultimately kept their subjects in check by the threat or use of force.

In addition, before the twentieth century, when empires dominated the planet and political inequality within, as well as among, sovereign states was both common and widely accepted, the word did not carry the stigma it came to bear in the second half of that century and thereafter. Thomas Jefferson looked forward to his countrymen creating an "empire of liberty" in North America.[49]

American rule in the Philippines fits the classical imperial template. The United States controlled the archipelago directly, without the consent of the people who lived there. In this way, and in violation of its dominant political ideas, America followed the pattern of the great European empires. Unlike the European imperial experiences, however, the American empire quickly became unpopular with Americans.[50] Unlike the European powers, the United States did not expand its imperial holdings.§ After 1898, whenever it occupied a foreign country it did so with the declared intention, which was always fulfilled, of turning responsibility for governing it over to the local people and leaving. A few years after the Spanish–American War, the American government committed itself to this very course in the Philippines, which, after two world wars, eventually became independent in 1946.[51]

The eminent diplomatic historian of the United States Samuel Flagg Bemis termed the American venture in the Philippines "a grand national aberration." Certainly, the imperial career of the United States does not compare, in scope or duration, with those of Great Britain, France, Spain, Portugal, the Netherlands, and even the latecomers to

---

§ The United States acquired other territories in 1898. Of these, the Teller Amendment, passed by the Congress, prohibited annexation of Cuba, although the subsequently enacted Platt Amendment made Cuba part of the American sphere of influence until the Castro revolution of the late 1950s. Hawaii eventually became the fiftieth state of the Union, and Puerto Rico assumed the status of a commonwealth, with some but not all of the privileges of statehood. Michael Mandelbaum, *The Four Ages of American Foreign Policy: Weak Power, Great Power, Hyperpower, Superpower*, New York: Oxford University Press, 2022, p. 146.

empire, Germany and Japan. Nor, after 1898, did Americans think of their country as an imperial power or attempt to acquire and maintain a formal empire.[52] International inequality does take a number of forms besides direct control of foreigners, however, to which, in recent years, the label "empire" has been affixed. The history of American foreign policy includes several of them.

Like classical imperialism, the expansion of the United States across North America in the first half of the nineteenth century involved the use of force and came at the expense of the indigenous peoples—the Native Americans, or Indians.[53] However, in its march westward and southward from the Atlantic Seaboard, America did not govern the territories it acquired and settled in the same way that the European powers governed their empires. Instead, as the result of the Northwest Ordinance of 1787, the new territories were incorporated into the Union as states of the United States, with all the rights and privileges enjoyed by existing states. In the British Empire, India did not have the same status as Lancashire; but Texas and California, when they entered the Union, did so as the equals of Massachusetts and Virginia.

As for the indigenous people, although the American treatment of them varied—it included efforts to uplift them but was frequently harsh and sometimes brutal[54]—they did ultimately gain full American citizenship, although until almost the end of the nineteenth century many preferred a separate, independent existence and were willing to fight to obtain it.[55] Still, while Indians in India could not vote to send Members of Parliament to London, Indians in the United States, despite their travails, ultimately could (and do) vote to send Members of Congress to Washington.

In addition to empires, powerful countries have acquired spheres of influence: geographically proximate regions where they exercise considerable economic and political influence but without direct, ongoing control. The United States acquired such a sphere in Central America and the eastern part of the Pacific Ocean, beginning in the final decades of the nineteenth century, which did resemble an empire in significant ways.[56] With the Roosevelt Corollary to the Monroe Doctrine, announced by Theodore Roosevelt in 1904, the United States claimed the right to arrange to its own satisfaction the internal affairs of the smaller, weaker countries to its south;[57] and it did periodically occupy several of them, ostensibly for that purpose. The justifications of these interventions made reference to the goals of humanitarian intervention and state-building,[58] and this was not merely empty rhetoric. The American presence did make contributions to the well-being of the people of Mexico, Cuba, and the Dominican Republic,[59] but it was also motivated by more self-serving goals such as collecting taxes and protecting property. With all of that, though, the United States did not claim the right, as imperial powers do, to govern these places directly and indefinitely.

The people who were subjected to America's formal empire, its westward expansion, and its sphere of influence, could not be said to have welcomed the relationships they were forced to have with the United States; and insofar as the Filipinos, the American Indians, and the Central Americans received benefits from their associations with America, these have to be weighed against the costs that they had to pay. In general, therefore, as the United States became more powerful, it did not always use its power in ways in keeping with the political ideas it was ostensibly, and most of the time actually, committed to disseminating beyond its borders.

In the case of another, more recent episode of international inequality involving the United States, however, the balance between advantage and disadvantage for American values, both in historical perspective and in the eyes of those affected by it, comes out more positively. In Western Europe and East Asia after 1945, the United States held a position of hegemony. The word "hegemony" comes from the Greek and means "preeminence" and "leadership."[60] America emerged from World War II far stronger than the countries of these regions, and it used its strength to provide political and economic leadership and military protection to these countries. The weaker countries, some of which had been America's adversaries in the war, accepted what the United States offered, and did so willingly, indeed sometimes gratefully. Insofar as the postwar arrangements amounted to an American empire, it was an "empire by invitation."[61] Because the United States both protected democracy and encouraged its spread in these two regions, in its capacity as hegemon it was faithful to the ideology of American foreign policy. Hegemony, to a far greater extent than its empire, its continental expansion, or its sphere of influence, advanced the ideas that the United States sought to promote beyond its own borders.

At roughly the time that the country began to assert itself internationally, the idea of arbitration between countries at odds with each other for the purpose of preventing or terminating wars achieved a measure of international acceptance. Two conferences on the conduct of war took place at The Hague in the Netherlands in 1899 and 1907, and from them emerged principles for bringing about and maintaining peace that included the voluntary arbitration of disputes. Peace being a fundamental precept of the ideology of American foreign policy, the idea of mediating between countries in conflict appealed to American leaders,[62] who adopted it as their own.

President Theodore Roosevelt undertook two efforts at mediation, both of which bore fruit. In the wake of the Russo–Japanese War of 1905, he brought representatives of the two countries to Portsmouth, New Hampshire, and, although not present in person, acted as the guiding spirit in reaching a settlement between them. In addition, he helped to convene a conference at Algeciras in Spain in 1906 that smoothed over a dispute between France and Germany over the French role in Morocco.[63]

Subsequent presidents and other American officials followed in Roosevelt's footsteps. During both world wars, before the United States entered the fighting, the president at the time—Woodrow Wilson in the first case, Franklin Roosevelt in the second—sent trusted envoys to Europe to try to mediate between the belligerent powers, albeit without success. In the wake of the Second World War, President Harry Truman dispatched General George Marshall to China in an effort to end the civil war there between Chiang Kai-shek's Nationalists and Mao Zedong's Communists, a mission that also failed.[64] In 1973, prompted by a war between Israel and its Arab neighbors, the United States began efforts to broker an end to their conflict, an enterprise that continued well into the twenty-first century. That ongoing effort did yield peace treaties between Israel and Egypt as well as between Israel and Jordan.[65]

Mediation offered a way to promote peace in particular parts of the world by resolving specific disputes. The ideology of American foreign policy, and the public officials who embraced it and were charged with carrying out the country's relations with other countries, had loftier ambitions than that. One of them launched a serious effort to implement a grand design for abolishing war altogether. The opportunity for this project, a milestone in the history of American foreign policy and indeed of international relations more generally, came about because of the most destructive war the world had yet seen.

THE ERA OF THE TWO WORLD WARS, 1914–1945

Woodrow Wilson, the twenty-eighth president of the United States, stands out in American history as the avatar of the country's ideological foreign policy. So closely did he become identified with it that the ideological approach has come to be known as "Wilsonianism."[66] The term is misleading in the sense that Wilson did not found that approach: he inherited it. The desire to export liberal ideas and practices is an American tradition, not a Wilsonian invention. Thomas Jefferson, an important American revolutionary and the nation's third president, believed as deeply in the propagation of American political ideas beyond North America as did Wilson.[67]

Of all Jefferson's successors, however, Wilson was perhaps the most strongly committed to this kind of foreign policy, in part by reason of his personal background. As the son of a Presbyterian minister, the tenets of the Protestant religion that did so much to shape American political culture loomed large in his life. In politics he belonged to the Progressive Movement and devoted his single term as governor of New Jersey, and then the domestic side of his presidency, to legislation designed to modernize American institutions in order to make them suitable for a country that had become far more urban and industrial since its founding.[68] His impulse to improve international affairs was in keeping with this ethic of improvement and adaptation. He brought the spirit of reform to the global arena.

Woodrow Wilson became the embodiment of ideology in foreign policy as well because he happened to be president at the moment when the world became more receptive than ever before to American ideas, particularly the desirability and feasibility of peace.[69] World War I, with the terrible death and destruction that it wreaked, made the reconstruction of international politics, by abandoning Europe's age-old practice of *realpolitik* in the interest of avoiding another such conflagration, seem imperative. Wilson had a plan for reconstruction, one rooted in the American ideological tradition, and he brought it to the postwar peace conference held at Paris in 1919. There, he commanded considerable authority, at least initially, because of the global demand for what he hoped to achieve. Wilson arrived at Paris in a position of substantial influence for another reason: by virtue of having funded the British war effort prior to 1917, and then having entered the war on the side of the Allies and given them victory by tipping the military balance in their favor, the United States had established itself as a major power in the world. As such, the American president's views on the postwar world counted for a great deal.

When the war began, most Americans preferred to stay out of it. Some who followed foreign affairs closely, a few of them serving in the Wilson administration, actively favored the British and French side. They did so for an ideological reason: those two countries had more democratic political systems than did the German, Habsburg, and Ottoman Empires they were fighting (although France and Britain's ally Russia had, if anything, a more autocratic government than the members of the opposing coalition). The United States had a realist motive as well: an Allied defeat would overturn the European balance of power and give Germany a dominant position on the Continent.[70] Wilson wanted to keep the United States out of the conflict almost from the beginning, but regarded World War I as an opportunity to realize a long-standing American goal, one to which he had developed a deep commitment: the abolition of war itself. On January 22, 1917, before the United States entered the conflict, he called for a "peace without victory."

While officially neutral, Wilson's country did provide considerable assistance to the Allies, and in particular to Great Britain, through expanded trade and American loans. Britain's Royal Navy controlled the Atlantic Ocean and thus could protect North American trade with the British Isles while blocking it with Germany. To counteract what was for them a serious disadvantage, the Germans began using a new weapon of war, the submarine, to sink ships, including passenger vessels, sailing between Britain and North America.[71] This practice ultimately brought the United States into the war.

Americans, including President Wilson, deemed submarine warfare a glaring violation of international law and in particular a violation of America's rights as a neutral party.[72] They demanded that Germany put an end to it, and for a time the Germans did. They resumed it at the beginning of 1917, and in April of that year the United States declared war on Germany. Wilson's war message to Congress justified entering the conflict on the grounds that "the right is more precious than peace." He offered a list of goals for the war that drew on the canon of American political ideas.[73] The United States waged World War I, therefore, for ideological reasons, among others.

The next year, on January 8, 1918, in an address to the Congress, Wilson set out American war aims in greater detail. He had not consulted America's allies in devising them. His "Fourteen Points" speech drew on the ideas that Americans had long sought—usually, to be sure, through the force of their example—to implement worldwide. Wilson recommended, in Points VII through XIII, specific territorial changes in Europe so that the countries affected would be composed of single nations.[74] He also advocated open diplomacy, free trade, the reduction of armaments, and the formation of "a general association of nations to guarantee independence and territorial integrity for all sovereign states."

At the peace conference held in Paris after the war ended, Wilson attempted to incorporate these ideas into the postwar settlement, with two of them receiving particular emphasis. Out of the three defeated multinational empires were carved independent nation-states, which were intended to be faithful to the American preference that sovereignty be apportioned, and borders drawn, according to the national principle. In addition, Wilson took the lead in designing the association of sovereign states for which he had called. That idea had other proponents,[75] not all of them Americans, but without Wilson's strong support it would have been unlikely to achieve the prominence it did in the wake of the war. In Paris, the United States had the opportunity, or so it seemed, to remake the international order according to American political ideas, and Wilson was determined to seize that opportunity.

The Wilsonian project of transforming international relations achieved at best partial success. Implementing its two most salient ideas turned out to be difficult. The successor states to the defeated empires were not all composed of a single nation. Instead, some groups found themselves in new countries dominated by others, which led to discontent and worse. A large number of Germans, for example, were assigned to countries dominated by other nationalities rather than to Germany. Hitler used the goal of bringing all Germans into a single state as a justification for the aggressive policies he launched in the 1930s, which led to World War II. Moreover, while the Czechs, Hungarians, and Romanians among others received sovereign states of their own, the non-European inhabitants of the empires of the victorious powers, Great Britain and France, did not. Those two countries kept, indeed expanded, their imperial holdings, and Wilson did not seriously challenge them on this point. Their empires continued to exist until after the Second World War.

As for the League of Nations, America's allies, especially France, were not willing to entrust their security to it. The French prime minister, Georges Clemenceau, had little use for an international organization to keep the peace, placing his faith, instead, in a different, long-standing feature of international relations. He told the French chamber of deputies that "There is an old system of alliances called the Balance of Power—this system of alliances, which I do not renounce, will be my guiding thought at the Peace Conference."[76]

Moreover, despite Wilson's deep personal commitment to it, the United States Senate rejected American membership in the League of Nations. That rejection had several causes, among them the stubborn, maladroit political campaign that Wilson himself waged on behalf of the organization until suffering an incapacitating stroke in October 1919. The League failed to win approval for another reason: Article X of its covenant seemed to obligate League members to come to the aid of any other member victimized by external aggression.[77] Such an obligation was inconsistent with the American Constitution, which reserved to the United States Senate the power to declare war. Most senators were not willing to take so radical a step. Wilson never offered a satisfactory explanation of the meaning of Article X. He said that it entailed a moral but not a legal obligation, which hardly clarified the matter.[78]

Despite the problems that its main features raised, and despite the fact that another, even more destructive, war broke out twenty years later, some aspects of the postwar settlement nonetheless endured. Most of the borders that emerged from the peace conference remained intact more than one hundred years later. In addition, after the Second World War the victors established a successor organization to the League, the UN, which the United States did join.

More generally, although his ideas were far from fully implemented, and where implemented were less than entirely successful, these ideas lived on after Wilson passed from the scene and indeed gained in popularity. Over time, other countries adopted them. The foreign policy of Europe in its various stages of integration, culminating in the European Union, to which France and Germany as well as, for a time, Great Britain belonged, can be called Wilsonian. The credit for Europe's transformation does not, to be sure, belong to Wilson personally. It was two massively costly world wars that turned Europeans against war and empire and instilled in them a powerful respect for individual liberty.

Wilson's ideas have lived on, as well, in the foreign policy of the United States,[79] although their persistence has less to do with admiration of the twenty-eighth president than with the fact that the commitment to liberty, democracy, and peace is so deeply embedded in American political culture. Almost all of his successors have at least paid lip service to these ideas, and most have gone further and tried in some way to put them into practice.

While the career of Woodrow Wilson demonstrated the difficulties of conducting an ideological foreign policy, subsequent American history also demonstrated that as long as the United States disposed of great international power, it would not content itself with passively offering the world an example of liberal institutions and practices. It would undertake active efforts to spread them beyond its borders.

Disillusioned by the results of World War I, in the interwar period the United States withdrew from engagement in the security affairs of Europe into which the war had drawn it. America did, however, take an active part in the international politics of the Asia-Pacific region. It launched an initiative in 1921, born of one of the precepts of the ideology of American foreign policy, that brought, if not lasting peace, then at least a temporary measure of stability to the region.

In 1921, Secretary of State Charles Evans Hughes convened a meeting in Washington to discuss limits on the warships that the principal naval powers in the Pacific deployed. The Washington Conference produced three closely related treaties: the Five-Power Treaty set a ratio in battle-ship tonnage among the United States, Great Britain, Japan, France, and Italy. The Four-Power Treaty involved an agreement among the United States, Britain, Japan, and France to respect the Pacific possessions of all the others and to consult with one another in the event of a threat to any of them. Under the terms of the Nine-Power Treaty, other European imperial powers joined signatories of the Five-Power Treaty in pledging not to encroach on China's sovereignty or territorial integrity.[80]

Through the Washington accords, the major powers voluntarily agreed to restrict their weaponry, a measure almost without precedent.[81] In the United States and elsewhere, the treaties raised the expectation, or at least the hope, that they would lead to further disarmament and that by disarming, governments would put an end to the institution of warfare.[82] That is not what happened. The agreements were in fact an in-stance of the familiar realist method of avoiding war through a balance of military power among potential adversaries. None of the adherents to the treaties imagined that it would relinquish all of their weaponry. Each calculated that contriving a maritime equilibrium among them served its particular interests at the time of signing. Still, the treaties did have an impact. It prevented a naval arms race in the Pacific and froze, for a time, the political status quo there.[83]

They thus validated, in a modest way, the American idea that putting limits on armaments could help to preserve peace. The Washington

Treaties therefore count as a success for the ideological foreign policy of the United States. The success did not last. Japan decided to challenge the existing distribution of power and territory in Asia. Its challenge destroyed the political foundation on which the treaties rested and paved the way for World War II in Asia.

The United States had the same initial reaction to the Second World War as to the First: a desire to remain aloof from the fighting. President Franklin D. Roosevelt, however, was far more openly sympathetic to Britain and France, and hostile to Germany, than Woodrow Wilson had been. When America did enter the war, after the Japanese attack on Pearl Harbor, Hawaii, on December 7, 1941, it had both realist and ideological motives for doing so. The domination of Europe at which Germany aimed and had all but achieved, and Japanese control of the Pacific, which also came close to being realized, posed serious threats to the security of the United States, and Roosevelt said so.[84] At the same time, the country was fighting to defend its own political ideas: its two principal adversaries celebrated war, sought to establish and maintain empires that brutally suppressed the national aspirations of the people they conquered, had no regard for individual liberty either in their own countries or elsewhere, and in Hitler's case murdered six million of the Jewish people.

To underscore the ideological character of the war, in August 1941, Franklin Roosevelt issued, jointly with the British prime minister Winston Churchill, a statement comparable to Wilson's Fourteen Points. It, too, set out war aims, even though the United States had not yet formally entered the conflict.[85] What came to be known as the Atlantic Charter opposed territorial conquest and endorsed, among other precepts, self-government, international cooperation, and disarmament.[86]

The American government was able to mobilize the entire country for the war effort over four years in no small part because Americans understood that they were fighting not only for geopolitical advantage—or more accurately to avoid geopolitical disaster—but also in defense of the political ideas that defined their public life. Victory in that war protected those ideas in other countries as well as putting an end to serious threats to the United States.

THE COLD WAR, 1945–1990

With the end of World War II in 1945, the coalition that won the war broke apart and its two principal members, the United States and the Soviet Union, became adversaries. They prosecuted their rivalry by every means available to them except direct military conflict, hence the name for that rivalry—the Cold War. The Cold War dominated American foreign policy, and indeed all of international politics, until the final decade of the twentieth century.

Like the two world wars, the Cold War was a contest of power, and the military standoff between the two sides in Europe constituted a twentieth-century version of a balance of military power. In addition to its realist character, though, America's rivalry with the Soviet Union also had a major ideological component. Not solely a contest of power, it was also a conflict between distinctive and radically different political and economic systems. The United States and the Soviet Union each led a group of politically and economically similar countries that functioned both as military coalitions and ideologically homogeneous communities.

While the political system of the United States and most of its allies was based on liberty and national independence, the Soviet Union and the coalition that it led suppressed all three forms of liberty—political, economic, and religious—and forcibly kept the nations of Central and Eastern Europe, the Caucasus, and Central Asia subordinate to Russian communist domination. The West, as America and its allies came to be called, organized economic life according to free-market principles, the common denominator of which is economic liberty. The communist world operated "command" economies in which the government made all major decisions and imposed them from above on the society.

Each side regarded its system as universally valid. Each believed the world was destined to adapt its political and economic institutions and practices. The communist conviction that the immutable laws of history dictated the ultimate worldwide triumph of the suite of political and economic ideas known as Marxism–Leninism matched the evangelical cast of America's liberal ideology. This meant that neither side could or did regard the other's system as legitimate or permanent.

In waging the Cold War, the United States was, among other things, conducting an ideological foreign policy, as President Harry Truman made clear in announcing what became known as the Truman Doctrine, the rough equivalent for the Cold War of the Fourteen Points for World War I and of the Atlantic Charter for World War II.

"At the present moment in world history," he said, "nearly every nation must choose between alternative ways of life." "One way of life," he continued,

> [I]s based upon the will of the majority and is distinguished by free institutions, representative government, free elections, guarantees of individual liberty, freedom of speech and religion, and freedom from political oppression. The second way of life is based upon the will of a minority forcibly imposed upon the majority. It relies upon terror and oppression, a controlled press and radio, fixed elections and the suppression of personal freedoms.[87]

Ideologically charged terminology suffused the language Americans used to describe the conflict. They referred to the West as "the free world" and the people involuntarily a part of the Soviet-dominated bloc in Eastern Europe as "captive nations." President Dwight D. Eisenhower, not a particularly ideologically inclined Cold War leader, said of the world and his country's place in it in his first inaugural address that "freedom is pitted against slavery; lightness against dark."[88] Ideological rhetoric reached its zenith in the inaugural address of his successor, John F. Kennedy, in which Kennedy vowed that the United States would "pay any price, bear any burden, meet any hardship, support any friend, oppose any foe to assure the survival and success of liberty."** American

---

** James M. Patterson, *Grand Expectations: The United States, 1945–1974*, New York: Oxford University Press, 1996, p. 486. Kennedy, the first Catholic president, was also the chief executive most committed to the Protestant-style evangelism of American political ideas. It was he who established the Peace Corps, the secular equivalent of the Protestant missionaries the United States began to send abroad in the second half of the nineteenth century.

schoolchildren recited the Pledge of Allegiance to the American flag, which, it said, represented a country that provided "liberty and justice for all."

A feature of the Cold War that distinguished it from previous international rivalries brought one particular American political idea to the fore of the great confrontation. World War II ended with the use, against the Japanese cities of Hiroshima and Nagasaki, of the most powerful weapon of war ever invented, the atomic bomb. The two Cold War rivals competed to develop and expand their stockpiles of these weapons, which drew their explosive force from the nucleus of matter. Their possession of these weapons gave them a common informal title: nuclear superpower. The unprecedentedly destructive potential of their nuclear arsenals gave rise to a worldwide demand for measures to ensure that atomic bombs would not be used again.

Early in the Cold War, therefore, each of the superpowers offered plans for "General and Complete Disarmament." These schemes to rid the world of all armaments were intended principally to advertise American and Soviet good intentions rather than to serve as blueprints for the countries of the world to follow.[89] Beginning in 1972, however, the two countries did reach agreements on modest limits on some of the several thousand nuclear weapons they had built and deployed.[90]

While the nuclear agreements were the result of the same impulse to reduce the possibility of war by reducing the weapons of war that had animated the Washington Treaties of the interwar period, they differed from the earlier agreements in that they were bilateral—involving only the United States and the Soviet Union—rather than multilateral. They differed as well in that, because the Soviet Union was a closed society, compliance with their terms had to be verified through reconnaissance by earth-orbiting satellites that only became available in the 1960s. Moreover, because they affected the two nuclear stockpiles at the margins, the later agreements had a lesser impact on the actual military balance than the earlier ones. In military terms, the earlier naval restraints were more significant than the nuclear limitations.

The two sets of arms restrictions also shared similar features. Like the Washington Treaties, the nuclear arms control agreements arose from political considerations. Like the naval accords, they became possible when the parties to them decided that their interests lay in maintaining, rather than attempting to overturn, the status quo—at least where nuclear weapons were concerned. The treaties of the 1970s differed from those of the 1920s, however, in that by negotiating them the two nuclear superpowers sought, among other goals, to reassure each other and the world that they recognized the extraordinary danger these weapons posed and that they would therefore exercise responsible stewardship of them.[91]

In the last stage of the Cold War, the political relationship between the two superpowers changed, and so, consequently, did the nature of the arms control accords they reached. At the end of the 1980s, the United States and the Soviet Union ceased to be the mortal rivals they had been since the latter part of the 1940s, which opened the way for agreements that actually reduced their stockpiles of weaponry, both nuclear and non-nuclear. Moreover, they adjusted the deployment of their military forces so as to make them suitable for defending but not conquering territory. This went beyond signaling prudence, which is what the earlier nuclear accords did; the later ones had a major impact on their military capabilities. In this way, the later nuclear accords did much more than had the earlier pacts to fulfill the original idea of reducing weaponry to promote peace. They reshaped the two military forces to make using them for aggressive purposes more difficult and war, therefore, less likely.[92]

In the Cold War, as in the two world wars, realism and ideology complemented and reinforced each other in the conduct of American foreign policy. By opposing aggressive, illiberal adversaries the United States was protecting American ideas and American interests at the same time. Still, the two approaches did not align on every issue. During the first half of the Cold War—a time when the Soviet threat seemed urgent—Americans were willing to set aside their ideological commitments for the sake of resisting the threat they faced. They had done the same during World War II, when, for the sake of defeating Nazi Germany, their country had made common cause with the same illiberal Soviet Union that subsequently became America's chief adversary. In the second half of the Cold War, however, the threat came to seem less pressing, and choosing realist over ideological policies provoked a political backlash. On some issues, some Americans made clear that they wanted a more ideological foreign policy—that is, in closer harmony with the nation's political ideas—than their government was conducting. In so doing they demonstrated the continuing political salience in the United States of the long-standing national commitment to disseminating these ideas abroad.

The nuclear arms agreements of the 1970s formed the heart of a wider policy toward the Soviet Union undertaken by President Richard Nixon and his chief foreign policy aide, Henry Kissinger. The policy came to be called détente, the French word for a relaxation of tensions. It aimed at regulating, although not ending, the superpower competition by reducing its intensity and thus lightening the political and economic burden that prosecuting the Cold War placed on the United States.[93]

For the sake of moderating the competition with the rival superpower, Nixon and Kissinger—in the twentieth century the two senior American policymakers most committed to the practice of *realpolitik* at the expense of the country's liberal political ideas—were willing to ratify publicly what their predecessors in office had only tacitly accepted since the beginning of the Cold War: the division of Europe into two spheres of influence, with the countries to the east of West Germany consigned to the rule of communist parties that answered to the Soviet Union. The policy of détente also accepted that, despite the initial American advantage in nuclear weaponry, the Soviet Union had reached, and would maintain, nuclear parity with the United States.

While initially popular, the pursuit of détente ultimately aroused opposition of two kinds. Some opponents based their objections on realist considerations. The global balance of power, they believed, had shifted against the United States and, they were convinced, American foreign policy should seek to redress that balance rather than agreeing to freeze it in place.[94] Détente came in for ideological criticism as well, on the grounds that America should not accept the Soviet Union's illiberal practices or cooperate closely with the government that oversaw them. One such practice was a ban on emigration. A congressional measure sponsored by Senator Henry Jackson of Washington and Congressman Charles Vanik of Ohio, both Democrats and thus both political opponents of the Republican President Nixon, took aim at that practice by prohibiting expanded Soviet–American trade, which was part of the Nixon–Kissinger design for détente, unless Moscow permitted free emigration—something it refused to do.[95] The Jackson–Vanik Amendment demonstrated the enduring strength of the ideological approach to foreign policy in the United States.[96]

Further evidence of this strength came from another domestic political conflict, this one over the proper policy toward governments that aligned with the United States against the Soviet Union internationally but rejected American political ideas at home, governing in autocratic rather than democratic fashion. American administrations had given political, economic, and military support to these so-called Friendly Tyrants[97] in order to fortify the American position in the Cold War. In the 1980s, support for two such autocrats—Antonio Somoza, the dictator of Nicaragua, and the Shah of Iran, a Middle Eastern ally of the United States—became politically controversial. The domestic criticism of Washington's alignment with them once again demonstrated the continuing demand among Americans for fidelity to the country's political ideas in its relations with other countries—that is, for an ideological foreign policy.[98]

Nicaragua and Iran did not turn out well for the United States and thereby served as cautionary lessons about the potential costs of such fidelity in the case of Friendly Tyrants. Both Somoza and the Shah fell from power, in part because of a lack of wholehearted American support. In each case, the successor regime proved to be both more tyrannical in its treatment of its people and actively *un*friendly to the United States.

In contrast to those two failures, during the course of the Cold War, America recorded the two most successful episodes of another ideological feature of its foreign policy: state-building. It did conspicuously better in installing its favored political and economic practices in its defeated World War II adversaries, Germany and Japan, than it had in the post–Civil War American South or the Philippines and Central

America in the early twentieth century—or, indeed, than it was able to do subsequently in other countries. With encouragement and some assistance from the United States, the defeated powers transformed themselves, in a remarkably short time, from aggressive dictatorships into stable, prosperous, peaceful, democratic American allies. (This was true of the western part of Germany, which became the German Federal Republic. The eastern part, occupied by the Soviet Union, became the emphatically illiberal German Democratic Republic.)

The two conditions that had hampered earlier state-building efforts were not present, at least not to the same extent, in post-1945 Germany and Japan. The United States did not withdraw its military forces from them. Indeed, the onset of the Cold War and the threat that the Soviet Union presented to both made American forces welcome, as they came to be seen by both Germans and Japanese as protectors rather than occupiers. The ongoing American military presence served as a hedge in both places against a reversion to political autocracy and aggressive foreign policies.

Of greater importance for their democratization was the fact that, by reason of demography and history, Germany and Japan were more receptive to, and better able to incorporate into the governance of their societies, the political ideas that the United States wished to export than had been the case in previous state-building exercises. Both had a more or less homogeneous population: Germany consisted almost exclusively of Germans, Japan of Japanese. The two thus avoided the kind of ethnic conflict that damaged the chances for stable democracy in other, more heterogeneous countries. In addition, each had had some experience with representative government before World War II, so democracy was not an entirely alien political system. Each also had developed the institutions of a free-market economy, whose revival after the war rapidly made Germany and Japan prosperous. Prosperity, in turn, helped to cement public allegiance to liberal political ideas in both places.

In contrast to these successes, American state-building suffered a signal failure in South Vietnam, where a war with communist North Vietnam severely handicapped the construction of stable institutions.[99] The North won the war in 1975 and forcibly incorporated non-communist

South Vietnam into its communist state through occupation, coercion, and the flight of many Vietnamese unsympathetic to the new masters.

The end of the Cold War, finally, represented the triumph—albeit indirectly—of American political ideas, perhaps the greatest success of the country's ideological foreign policy in all of American history. The outcome of the Soviet–American conflict resembled the results of the two world wars. Like Germany in the wake of both conflicts, the losing side, the Soviet Union, relinquished territory and adopted—or at least, in the case of post-Soviet Russia, tried for a time to adopt—the political system of the victor. Unlike the two previous conflicts, however, the Soviet–American rivalry was not decided on the battlefield. Between its two major antagonists the Cold War never became hot. The Soviet Union and the communist governments of Central and Eastern Europe collapsed from within;[100] and to this collapse the idea and the practice of liberty in both politics and economics, as well as the aspiration to national self-government in the territories where communism held sway, made substantial contributions.

For in the contest of systems at the heart of the Cold War, the Western system, which embodied liberal ideas, proved superior to the communist one. It delivered a higher standard of living and commanded deeper allegiance among the people living under it. In an effort to match the Western performance, the Soviet leader Mikhail Gorbachev introduced reforms that, contrary to his intention, caused the communist order in Europe to disintegrate. The peoples of Eastern Europe peacefully overthrew the communist governments that had been imposed on them after World War II, and, in acts of national self-determination, escaped from the Soviet empire. Then the Soviet Union itself broke apart and the governments of the successor states rejected orthodox communism.

In these events, American foreign policy reverted to a nineteenth-century pattern. The American example, not direct American intervention, helped bring down European communism; and the American example had the powerful impact that it did because it was not solely an American one. The countries of Western Europe had put liberal ideas into practice and had thrived. This made a deep impression on the people to the east, an impression that turned out to be decisive for the future of the continent. The Cold War triumph was an American as well as a European one, however. America's European allies had adopted liberal political ideas in no small part because of the efforts and the example of the United States, which remained their most prominent exemplar and evangelist; and it was these ideas that won the Cold War.

THE POST–COLD WAR ERA, 1990–2015

The demise of communism in Europe ushered in a golden age of the American ideological approach to foreign policy in the sense that, as a governing principle of America's relations with the rest of the world, it had no serious competition. The United States did not have to give priority to defending its security as it had in the past because, with the disappearance of the Soviet Union, threats to its security had evaporated. America faced no major challenger. Historically, rivalries among several great powers have dominated international politics. During the Cold War there had been two such powers. With the disintegration of the Soviet Union only one remained. This freed the United States to devote whatever resources and attention it chose to reserve for foreign policy to the international promotion of its own political ideas.[101]

Policy toward China exemplified this change. During the Cold War, realist considerations defined that policy. From the communist victory in the Chinese Civil War until 1972, the American government regarded China, a Soviet ally rhetorically committed to fomenting communist revolutions around the world, as a serious military and political adversary. After the 1972 rapprochement with the regime in Beijing engineered by Nixon and Kissinger, the United States treated China as an ally in the confrontation with the Soviet Union.

Then, with the end of the Cold War, and in response to the ruling Communist Party's violent suppression in June 1989 of peaceful demonstrators—some of them advocating democratic political reform—in the capital, Beijing, and other cities, America's China policy shifted to an emphasis on human rights.[102] The first presidency to take place entirely in the post–Cold War era, that of Bill Clinton, made

American trade with China, which had flourished beginning in the early 1980s as a result of Chinese free-market reforms, contingent on respect by the communist government for the individual liberties of its citizens. That government, remaining true to Marxism–Leninism, refused to fulfill this requirement. Clinton then proceeded to reverse American policy. He pivoted to endorsing rather than opposing expanded trade with China. The wishes of American businessmen eager to do business in China no doubt had a great deal to do with his decision, but he justified it on the ideological grounds that more rather than less trade would foster Western-style political practices and institutions there.

Not only in its post–Cold War policy toward China, but with other countries as well, the United States sought to encourage the adoption of institutions embodying its own political ideas, above all democracy. President George W. Bush demonstrated the importance he imputed to democracy-promotion abroad by devoting his second inaugural address, in January 2009, to the subject. The inclination toward such an enterprise, embedded in America's political genes,[103] gathered strength from one of the signal features of late-twentieth-century global history. Democratic governments, a minor presence in the world at the founding of the United States, spread rapidly in Europe, Asia, and Latin America in the last quarter of the century. By one count, whereas in 1900 only ten countries qualified as democracies, by 2005 fully 119 of the world's 190 sovereign states met democratic standards.[104]

Buoyed by the tangible evidence that history was moving in their own preferred direction, Americans actively encouraged, through official rhetoric and modest stipends, the installation of governments chosen by popular sovereignty and committed to the protection of liberty in all its forms not only in China—where the Communist Party maintained a monopoly of political power—but also, explicitly, in newly non-communist Russia and in the autocratically governed Arab countries.

By the time the return of great-power rivalry in the middle of the second decade of the new century ended the golden age of ideology in American foreign policy,[105] none of these countries had become a full-fledged democracy. The allure of liberty turned out to be less potent than the political developments of the last quarter of the twentieth century had made it appear to Americans. Moreover, the dictatorial governments, such as the one in China, that the United States had hoped would be replaced by freely and fairly elected ones, resisted yielding their power. Because they controlled the armed forces and organs of security and did not hesitate to use them to repress challenges to their authority, their resistance prevailed.[106] Mao Zedong once asserted that political power grew out of the barrel of a gun. In China, Russia, and the Arab world, at least, that proved to be very much the case, even in the face of what seemed to be a powerful global political tide that Americans hoped would sweep autocracies away.

After the Cold War, the United States became far more deeply involved in a different set of countries, on behalf of another ideological foreign policy aim: the protection of people whose governments were assaulting them. America undertook military interventions for humanitarian rather than power-political purposes in Somalia, Haiti, Bosnia, and Kosovo—the last two previously parts of Yugoslavia, a communist multinational state that broke apart at the end of the 1980s.[107]

The United States used its armed forces in each case not for the traditional, realist purpose of securing America's interests but in order to defend the human rights of non-Americans. In the nineteenth century, with the exception of Cuba in 1898, while the American government had expressed its displeasure at what it regarded as the mistreatment of foreigners by their rulers, it had done nothing about what it deplored.[108] In the last decade of the twentieth century, by contrast, it deployed its armed forces to put a stop to such mistreatment. What had changed was America's relative power in the world. In the wake of the Cold War, the United States retained the formidable military forces it had amassed during the course of that conflict, but now no other country had countervailing military forces of comparable strength; and the governments whose depredations America used its military to terminate mounted very modest resistance, or none at all.††

†† On humanitarian intervention, see Michael Mandelbaum, *Mission Failure: America and the World in the Post-Cold War Era*, New York: Oxford University Press, 2016, Chapter 2, and Mandelbaum, *The Four Ages of American Foreign Policy*, pp. 400–410. In connection

While it was the United States that took military action on behalf of beleaguered people in Africa, the Caribbean, and southern Europe, an appreciable number of non-Americans approved of what America did. The idea that the international community had a "responsibility to protect" such people gained currency, although it contradicted the basic principle of international law that prohibits one country from using force on the territory of another without the permission of the government of the second country—the classic definition of international aggression.[109] In 2005, the UN passed a resolution endorsing the responsibility to protect.[110]

The humanitarian interventions of the 1990s did save some lives but did not prove popular with the American public: the most effective opposition to them came from within the United States. While in favor, in principle, of protecting the vulnerable abroad, the public was unwilling to spend American lives for that purpose. It approved of good deeds but did not approve of paying for them, at least not in blood. The Clinton administration prosecuted its humanitarian interventions while following the unwritten rule that the maximum number of allowable American fatalities was zero. While other democracies generally supported what the United States was doing, their support did not extend to supplying combat forces of their own for the humanitarian military operations. Nor did every country in the world accept the doctrine of "responsibility to protect" as a new and binding international norm. Notably, Russia and China did not accept it,[111] insisting on the continuing validity of what the doctrine rejected: the inviolability of national sovereignty.

As a result of its humanitarian interventions, the United States found itself occupying the places where it had intervened and thus saddled with the responsibility for governing them. True to its ideology, it sought to provide them with the institutions of modern, competent, democratic government.[112] In none of the four did state-building produce anything

with Somalia, the American ambassador to the United Nations, Madeleine Albright, made perhaps the most expansive statement by any public official in the nation's history of the ideological approach to foreign policy: "The United States has an inescapable responsibility to build a peaceful world and terminate the abominable injustices and conditions that still plague civilization." Quoted in *Mission Failure*, p. 75.

like the successful outcomes the United States had assisted in bringing about in post–World War II Germany and Japan. The two most serious, costly, and frustrating American attempts at state-building came later, however. They took place in the first decade of the twenty-first century in two countries that the United States had come to occupy after wars waged for realist, not ideological reasons: Afghanistan and Iraq.

Terrorist attacks on New York City and Washington, DC, on September 11, 2001, caused the American government to send troops to those two countries. The United States attacked them because the terrorists had their base in Afghanistan and because, after September 11, the George W. Bush administration became persuaded that Saddam Hussein, the dictator of Iraq, posed a serious threat and had to be removed from power.[113] Once in military control of each, the Bush administration had a choice: it could withdraw American troops, leaving the countries to whatever fate the struggle among their internal forces that would inevitably follow would produce. Or it could remain and, in keeping with the ideological tradition of the nation's foreign policy, try to build a stable, rights-protecting, peace-respecting government. In both cases it chose the second option.

The state-building in Afghanistan and Iraq failed, foundering on the same obstacles that had foiled similar efforts in the American South after the Civil War and in South Vietnam in the 1960s and 1970s. In all four places, state-building had to proceed in the midst of armed opposition. The insurrections against the American-sponsored governments in Afghanistan and Iraq interfered, to put it mildly, with the efforts to construct working institutions, as had the violent resistance to Reconstruction in the American South and the North Vietnamese campaign against the South. An active war zone is not a promising building site.

State-building in Afghanistan and Iraq—as in Bosnia, Somalia, Haiti, and Kosovo—suffered from other ultimately crippling hardships as well. Unlike Germany and Japan, they lacked a homogeneous population. They were composed of more than one tribe—or ethnic or linguistic or religious group—which were not disposed to coexist peacefully in a single political order underpinned by a universally applied legal code. More importantly, unlike Germany and Japan, they lacked the historical experience and the political values on which the kind of political and economic systems the United States was hoping to create must rest.[114] As the ancient Roman poet Horace observed, *Sine moribus legae vanae*: without the appropriate morals—meaning the ingredients of political culture—laws are in vain. Political culture cannot be imported from outside a society. It must be homegrown, and growing it takes generations.

Thus, the failure of state-building efforts in the post–Cold War era demonstrated the limits to America's ideological foreign policy. At its most ambitious, and when the United States stood at the apex of its power, the efforts to transfer American political ideas and institutions embodying them to other countries failed; and they failed because the tools of American foreign policy—what the United States, or any country, could do to, with, and within other countries—were inadequate. The United States could not make other countries over according to its preferred designs: only these countries themselves could do that. Thus, this type of initiative, stemming from America's foreign-policy ideology— the American mission of post–Cold War liberal transformation—ended in failure.

By 2015, the post–Cold War era had come to an end. With its end came the disappearance of the international conditions in which the United States had been able to conduct a foreign policy dominated by its political ideas while largely ignoring realist considerations of power and rivalry. The need to deal with other countries on the basis of power rather than ideas returned, with the rise of three countries bent on revising the political arrangements in their own regions to the detriment of America and its friends and allies: Russia in Europe, China in the Asia-Pacific area, and Iran in the Middle East.[115] The new world in which the United States had to operate more closely resembled the world of most of recorded history before the end of the Cold War, marked as it was by geopolitical rivalries and the constant threat of major war.

More specifically, this new world had far more in common with the four decades of the Cold War than with the quarter-century that followed that conflict's conclusion. To be sure, what might be called the post-post–Cold War era did differ from the period of the Soviet–American rivalry in three important ways. First, while during the Cold War the United States confronted a single adversary—the Communist bloc, with its headquarters in Moscow—in this new era it faced three different adversaries. The three cooperated with one another to some extent but each also acted independently. Second, while during the Cold War the communist countries stood almost entirely outside the American-led international economic order, the three twenty-first-century challengers participated in it, and China in particular played a major global economic role. American policy toward the revisionist powers therefore had to take economics into account in a way that it did not during the Cold War. Third, the challengers did not subscribe to a common, fully developed, radically anti-liberal ideology encompassing both politics and economics like the Marxism–Leninism of the Soviet Union. However, while their domestic political systems differed, Russia, China, and Iran all had authoritarian governments that rejected democratic principles and repressed democratic practices. They were all at odds, that is, with the liberal foreign-policy ideology of the United States.

In opposing the expansionist designs of the three, therefore, as in the two world wars and the Cold War, American foreign policy had an ideological dimension. At the beginning of his presidency, Joseph R. Biden made this explicit. Historians of the future, he said in March 2021, would be interested in "the issue of who succeeded: democracy or autocracy."[116] His administration proceeded to organize summit meetings of democratic countries in 2022 and 2023.

As during the Cold War, however, in this new era the United States found that, in dealing with other countries, its political ideas and its geopolitical interests did not always align. It sometimes had to choose between its values and its interests. As in the past, it usually gave priority to the protection of its interests. As in the Cold War, it chose to maintain good relations with undemocratic countries for the sake of effectively confronting its principal regional adversaries: still-communist

Vietnam in order to counterbalance China, for example, and autocratic Saudi Arabia for anti-Iranian purposes.[117]

In the quarter-century after the collapse of communism in Europe, the United States had been able to attempt to spread its own political ideas and institutions without giving serious attention to considerations of power politics. It had conducted the most ideological foreign policy in its history. With the return of great-power competition, it could no longer afford that luxury.

An Economic Foreign Policy

ECONOMICS AND POLITICS

Politics and economics, while conceptually distinct, are in practice always intertwined. In the world into which the independent American republic was born, the most powerful states used their power to generate wealth. They accumulated precious metals through trade surpluses and used these metals to purchase the services of mercenary soldiers, which enhanced their military power. They then employed that power to expand their wealth.[1] Specifically, they used their military power to acquire empires and created trade monopolies within their imperial domains that benefited them at the expense of their imperial subjects. This approach to politics and economics beyond their borders was known as mercantilism.[2]

The United States not only spurned mercantilism, it adopted the opposite practice. The distinctiveness of American foreign economic policies resides in the fact that the country has, more often than other sovereign states, reversed the mercantilist relationship by deploying economic instruments in pursuit of political goals. That predilection is a hallmark, and a distinctive feature, of the American approach to the world. In that particular sense, the United States has conducted an unusually economic foreign policy.

To be sure, the United States has not always deployed economic means for political ends. On occasion, like the mercantilist powers of history, it has used political and military initiatives for the purpose of making Americans wealthier. Its policies in East Asia in the second half of the nineteenth century—notably the opening of Japan for trade and the "Open Door" policy designed to preserve American economic access to China—fit this description.[*] In addition, the vast majority of the economic policies, domestic and international, that the United States has carried out since its founding, as is the case with other countries, have had economic rather than political purposes. Moreover, most of the economic policies the United States has carried out over the course of the country's history have had a domestic focus and have affected the economics or the politics of other countries only modestly and indirectly, if at all. Finally, while America has often had political goals for its economic initiatives, those economic initiatives have had economic aims as well: dual purposes and mixed motives have been consistently present.

Still, from the beginning, the United States has had, compared with all other sovereign states, a pronounced penchant for using economic instruments in pursuit of political goals. This has made American foreign policy, since the eighteenth century, different from the foreign policies of other countries.[3]

Why has American foreign policy been exceptional in this way? At its birth, the United States was too weak to carry out mercantilist policies, let alone acquire an empire to rival those of the European great powers. Moreover, the early Americans generally took a dim view of mercantilism, having been, as imperial subjects, its victims rather than its beneficiaries. Britain's mercantilist policies and laws, especially its seventeenth-century Navigation Acts, had imposed costs on the thirteen colonies; and although these did not prevent the colonies from becoming increasingly prosperous in the decades leading up to the Revolution,

---

[*] The two wars the United States launched against Iraq, in 1991 and 2003, had economic motives. The region's importance stemmed almost entirely from the large deposits of oil found there, on which the global economy depended in order to function smoothly. The political aims of the two Gulf Wars were just as important as the economic ones, however, if not more so. The United States went to war to prevent the Iraqi dictator, Saddam Hussein, from controlling a dangerously large share of the planet's petroleum resources for fear of the political uses to which he would put that control. The United States did not attempt to seize the region's oil fields for itself, which would have been the classical mercantilist approach.

this was in no small part the case because colonial merchants routinely ignored them.[4]

If the early Americans found mercantilism to be infeasible and uncongenial, the opposite approach, using economic instruments to achieve political goals, seemed, then and thereafter, likely to be effective.[5] That particular belief has persisted from the eighteenth century to the twenty-first. It stems ultimately from one of the fundamental features of American society.

Following the example of Great Britain, which Napoleon once derisively called "a nation of shopkeepers," Americans have placed commerce at the center of their national life from the beginning. The thirtieth American president, Calvin Coolidge, is often (not quite accurately) quoted as having said in 1925 that "the business of America is business."[6] This was true of the eighteenth and nineteenth centuries as well as the twentieth and twenty-first.[7] The colonies were founded as commercial enterprises,[8] and commercial agriculture dominated the colonial period and the early decades of independence: pioneers moved westward from the Atlantic coast in order to claim and work farmland and later land for ranching. The immigrants who have flocked to the United States since the eighteenth century have come in search of economic opportunity and have usually found it. Because economic considerations have loomed so large for Americans, they have assumed that such considerations have comparable importance for others and that the politics of other countries could therefore be swayed in directions the United States favored through the use of economic instruments.[9]

These economic instruments have come in two varieties. In the eighteenth and nineteenth centuries, America deployed the cross-border transfer of goods and services—trade—for political purposes. In the twentieth and twenty-first centuries, the international flow of money—capital in the form of loans, grants, and investments—joined trade as an instrument of American foreign policy.[10] The United States has wielded these two economic tools both as sticks and carrots—that is, as both punishments and as incentives.

The punitive use of economic instruments, usually taking the form of trade sanctions,[11] has a very long history in international affairs. Such sanctions have commonly been deployed in wartime, with the aim of degrading the enemy's military capacity and, by impoverishing its population, weakening its will to prosecute the conflict.[12]

The United States, in particular, has also employed economic sanctions in peacetime. Indeed, sanctions have often commended themselves to American policymakers as a substitute for war. In America's early years, when it was weak, it lacked viable military options for dealing with other states. Subsequently it became militarily powerful, but still often found the imposition of economic sanctions attractive as a way of imposing costs on other countries without placing American troops in harm's way.

In fact, the United States has sometimes imposed sanctions not in the expectation that these would force a change in the policies of foreign governments but rather as a way of expressing, at acceptable cost, American disapproval of those policies. In such cases, the target audience for the sanctions has included not only the countries being sanctioned but also Americans who wanted their government to take action of some kind against countries whose policies they found unacceptable.[13]

Sometimes sanctions have achieved their aims, although they have seldom induced other countries to alter their policies as extensively as the American sanctioners had hoped. Boycotts of British goods during the Revolutionary period did cause the revocation of some taxes to which the colonials objected, although this did not prevent the American break with the British Empire and the war it occasioned. More often, trade sanctions have failed to bring about the political changes Americans have sought: the target countries have deemed the policies that they were pursuing and that the United States was trying to stop sufficiently important to absorb whatever losses such sanctions inflicted.[14] Sanctioned countries have also often suffered less punishment than the United States intended because sanctions are rarely airtight. Target countries typically find ways to get around them by locating other sources of supply of whatever the sanctioning country or countries are attempting to deny to them.[15] Authoritarian regimes have proven especially resistant to sanctions.

On two notable occasions in the nineteenth century, during the Wars of the French Revolution and the Civil War, officials overestimated the impact that trade sanctions would have on Great Britain—then the richest country in the world—at considerable cost to the interests those officials sought to protect.[16] In carrying out international economic policies, the American government has also on occasion miscalculated and brought about the opposite result from the one it intended. A mishap of this kind occurred in connection with both world wars of the first half of the twentieth century.

As for economic incentives, those the United States has offered in pursuit of political goals have taken the form of access to the domestic American market and to American capital. These historically have been attractive inducements because, in the late nineteenth century, the American economy became the largest in the world. On the whole, the United States has done better with carrots than with sticks. Economic incentives in the form of access to trade and capital have had greater success in achieving American international goals than sanctions. This was especially the case during the period of the Cold War.

The sweep of American history exhibits a final pattern in the deployment of economic tools for political purposes. Over time, the United States has made ever-greater use of these tools, for two reasons. First, its rapid economic growth has given successive American governments expanding economic resources to deploy in pursuit of foreign policy goals. Second, and more generally, as the country has become richer and more powerful, the scope of its foreign policy has broadened. The episodes in which it has sought to influence the policies of others have multiplied, and the use of all the tools of foreign policy, including economic ones, has correspondingly expanded. More foreign policy has meant more occasions for using trade and finance, along with other methods of exerting influence, to affect what foreigners believe and do.

1765–1914

Americans used economic instruments to defend their interests even before they had an independent state. The rebellion against the British Empire had its roots in the colonials' objections to a series of taxes the British Parliament attempted to impose on them. The Americans responded by boycotting goods that British merchants were selling in the thirteen colonies, with the aim of putting pressure on those merchants so that they would in turn exert pressure on the British government to rescind the taxes. The tactic achieved some success. The British did cancel the Stamp Act of 1765 and the Townshend Acts of 1767.[17]

His Majesty's government sought to impose other economic obligations on its imperial subjects in North America,[18] however, and insisted on its right to do so. That right lies at the heart of sovereignty, and the war between Britain and the Americans that broke out in 1775 had at its core a dispute about who was sovereign in the colonies, Great Britain or the colonials themselves.[19] Such economic pressure as the Americans were able to bring to bear on British merchants did not suffice to persuade the British government to give up its own claim. Only war could—and eventually did—do that.

Several years after the war ended, the now-independent Americans adopted a constitution that gave their government more authority than it had wielded under the original governing document, the Articles of Confederation. The Constitution of 1788 specifically vested power over trade policy in the federal government, so as to make possible effective trade negotiations with other countries.[20] The framers of the Constitution were not thinking explicitly of using trade as a means of securing political goals; but by specifying and centralizing power over it, they gave subsequent American governments the opportunity to do so.

In fact, the newly independent United States aspired to trade as widely and as freely as possible.[21] The Wars of the French Revolution, which were fought between 1792 and 1815, frustrated that aspiration. Each of the two principal antagonists, Great Britain and France, adopted the familiar strategy of countries at war of trying to restrict the commerce of their adversary. This brought both into conflict with the United States, which wanted to do business with the whole world, including both Britain and France.

The administration of President John Adams settled the dispute with France with the Treaty of Mortefontaine of 1800. The conflict with Britain proved more difficult to resolve. During the administration of

President George Washington, who preceded Adams, the two countries agreed to a settlement of their differences in a 1794 treaty. That did not end the Anglo–American maritime conflict, however, and in 1812 the two went to war. In between these two events, there occurred an American initiative that ranks as one of the most remarkable, and least successful, uses of economic instruments for political purposes in all of American history—indeed one of the most remarkable and least successful American foreign policies of any kind: Thomas Jefferson's embargo.[22]

In 1807, Jefferson, who assumed the presidency after John Adams, imposed, through an act of Congress, a prohibition on all exports from the United States. No American ship was permitted to leave any port with cargo bound for any foreign country. Jefferson employed the tactic that countries at war had frequently used against their enemies, but in this instance against his own country. He believed that Great Britain had such great and pressing need for American products that cutting off British consumers from the United States would create enough pressure on the British government to compel it to cease the harassment of American ships and the seizure of their cargo and sailors.[23]

Jefferson had an additional motive. He wanted to show the world that embargoes could serve as effective methods of "peaceable coercion"[24] and thereby diminish the resort to armed conflict everywhere. He conceived of his embargo as a giant step toward the abolition of the age-old practice of war. His initiative thus belongs to the history of America's ideological foreign policies as well as its economic ones.

Events demonstrated that in this matter the third American president had seriously miscalculated. The embargo did not cause Great Britain to abandon the naval policies to which Americans objected. It provoked widespread evasion and inflicted serious economic and political damage on the United States itself. It cost the country an estimated 5 percent of its gross domestic product (GDP).[25] It also alienated many Americans: the people of New England, especially the region's merchants, strongly opposed Jefferson's measure, which became so unpopular with them that it stirred talk of secession.[26] This particular exercise in the employment of an economic instrument to change the policy of another country had emphatically failed by the time it was repealed in 1808, when Jefferson left office.[†] Its failure paved the way for the United States to try, in 1812, during the administration of Jefferson's successor, James Madison, to put an end to what it saw as Britain's illegal naval policies by war.

The War of 1812 ended in 1815, and between its end-point and the outbreak of the Civil War in 1861, trade policy became a major domestic political issue in the United States.[27] The question of tariffs on imports divided Americans by geographic region and economic sector.[28] Agriculture dominated the economy of the South, which sold abroad much of what it produced, especially cotton. Southerners therefore favored free trade. As the Industrial Revolution came to North America, much of the industrial activity in the United States, initially the manufacture of textiles, took place in the Northern states. Their products had to compete with those of Great Britain, against which Northerners sought protection through tariff barriers.[29] In this period, the South generally held the upper hand in national politics and thus was able largely to resist the North's demands for protection against foreign imports.

The Civil War furnished an occasion for another overestimation of the power of the economic tools of foreign policy. For the purpose of securing the independence for which it was fighting, the Confederacy placed great value on support from, or at least formal diplomatic recognition by, Great Britain. Britain's textile mills relied heavily on cotton grown in the American South, so the Confederacy implemented an informal cotton embargo to compel British assistance for its cause.[30]

The tactic worked no better for the secessionists than it had for Thomas Jefferson. Imports of cotton from the South plummeted,[31] but

[†] Henry Adams, in his *History of the United States During the Administrations of Jefferson and Madison* rendered this verdict on the embargo: "Financially it emptied the Treasury, bankrupted the mercantile and agricultural class, and ground the poor beyond endurance. Constitutionally, it overrode every specified limit on arbitrary power and made Congress despotic, while it left no bounds to the authority which might be vested by Congress in the President. Morally, it sapped the nation's vital force, lowering its courage, paralyzing its energy, corrupting its principles, and arraying all the active elements of society in factious opposition to the government or in secret paths of treason. Politically, it cost Jefferson the fruits of eight years painful labor for popularity, and it brought the Union to the edge of a precipice." Quoted in Robert W. Tucker and David C. Hendrickson, *Empire of Liberty: The Statecraft of Thomas Jefferson*, New York: Oxford University Press, 1990, p. 222.

Britain's textile industry coped successfully with the decline. A bumper cotton crop in the year before the war began gave the British a buffer stock of the commodity, which reduced the impact of the embargo; and as the conflict proceeded, the Lancashire textile mills found alternative sources, Egypt and India among them.

This enabled the British government to decide its policy toward the American Civil War on other grounds.[32] Despite some sympathy for the Confederacy and secession, in the end the British declined to side with the South because, among other reasons, important parts of the British public opposed the slavery the Southerners were fighting to preserve.[33] Moreover, in 1863 the tide of war turned against the South, and the British government did not want to be associated with the losing party in the conflict.

The outcome of the Civil War transformed the domestic politics of trade in the United States. The Union victory conferred political hegemony on the largely Republican Northern states, which favored protection; and from the mid-1860s until the Great Depression, when political dominance passed to the Democrats, the United States generally maintained tariff barriers against imports from abroad.[34] This made the imposition of economic sanctions for international political purposes problematical, since America was already restricting trade with the rest of the world, albeit for economic (and domestic political) reasons. Moreover, the revenues for the federal government came largely from tariffs, which also weighed against manipulating them in pursuit of political goals.[35]

Ironically, in the years between the Civil War and the end of the nineteenth century, despite Republican-inspired tariff barriers, the volume of American trade with the rest of the world actually increased. This was the result of the sharply falling costs of transporting goods across both water and land due to the increasing use of the steamship and the railroad.[36] In this period, the United States accumulated ever-greater potential economic leverage over other countries through the rapid economic growth it experienced. By the century's end, it had the largest economy in the world.[37]

In the early years of the twentieth century, two reforms enacted through the efforts of the Progressive Movement, although undertaken for other reasons, also enhanced the potential for deploying economic instruments to achieve political goals. In 1913, the Sixteenth Amendment to the Constitution authorized the taxation of incomes, which became the major source of the revenues that the federal government needed to operate. This decreased reliance on tariffs, and thus made it easier to forgo them should the country, for political or economic reasons (or both), decide to do so. That, in turn, paved the way for the use of the prospect of access to the American market as an incentive, which the United States did to good effect in the second half of the twentieth century. Also in 1913, the creation of the Federal Reserve put the American financial system on a more solid footing, which strengthened the potential for wielding capital—dollars—for political ends. Indeed, by that year the federal government was already doing so.

Until the twentieth century, the American use of economic instruments for political purposes had consisted of trade sanctions against Great Britain in conditions of war or near-war at the beginning of the American Revolution; by the administration of Thomas Jefferson in the middle years of the Wars of the French Revolution; and by the Confederacy at the outset of the Civil War. In 1912, the country inaugurated a new way of seeking political ends by economic means.

President William Howard Taft and his secretary of state, Philander Knox, devised a policy they called "Dollar Diplomacy."[38] It encouraged Americans to invest in places where the United States had political and economic interests—the countries of Central America and China—with the goal of contributing to political stability there and thus avoiding the need for military intervention: the United States had previously sent troops to Central America on several occasions and had joined the European great powers in intervening in China to put down the Boxer Rebellion of 1900. The hope of substituting "dollars for bullets" inspired the initiative.

With the growth of the American economy, access to American capital as well as to the American market became desirable to other countries. Dollar Diplomacy was designed to take advantage of that development. It relied entirely on private capital rather than funds from the government (and therefore the taxpayers). It had very modest effects, insofar as it had any effects at all, on the target countries. Its significance lies, rather, in the precedent it set. For the first time, the United States wielded money in pursuit of its political goals; and for the first time it deployed an economic instrument as an incentive rather than a punishment. Both would play significant roles in American foreign policy in the twentieth century and beyond, although less so in the period that immediately followed, the era of the two world wars.

THE ERA OF THE TWO WORLD WARS, 1914–1945

War dominated the years between 1914 and 1945, and thus the most important instrument of America's relations with other countries in that time was its armed forces. In this period, however, the international economic policy of the United States played a major, underappreciated, inadvertent part in its foreign policy. Specifically, international economic initiatives were responsible in no small part—and entirely unintentionally—for drawing the United States, which had tried to stay out of the fighting in both conflicts, into the two world wars.

When the First World War began, in 1914, America declared its neutrality. The country's neutral rights, the American government asserted, included, as in the Wars of the French Revolution, the right to trade with all parties. Trade between the United States and Great Britain and its allies France and Russia did increase sharply, to the great benefit of the American economy. So important did the transatlantic trade become for American prosperity[39] that the administration of President Woodrow Wilson authorized what it had initially prohibited as incompatible with neutrality, namely the floating of private American loans to the British so that they could sustain the volume of purchases they were making in the United States.[40]

American commerce with Great Britain and its allies created problems with Britain's principal wartime adversary, Imperial Germany.

The United States had no principled objection to doing business with the Germans as well as the British, but this proved infeasible because Britain's Royal Navy dominated the Atlantic Ocean and so could prevent shipping from reaching the countries against which Britain was fighting. Britain, France, and Russia therefore had economic access to the United States while Germany and its allies did not.[41] The United States was conducting a policy toward the belligerent parties that was de jure—legally—a neutral one; but de facto—in actual terms—that policy tilted sharply toward the British and French.

Germany sought to counteract the British advantage through the use of the recently invented submarine. The German practice of using its fleet of submarines—known as U-boats—to sink ships carrying cargo across the Atlantic outraged Americans, who came to regard this as a violation of their neutral rights and of the laws of war as well as an act of barbarism. The sinking of the passenger liner *Lusitania* on May 7, 1915, in which 1,198 people perished, including 128 Americans, made a particularly strong—and strongly negative   impression on American public opinion.[42] The United States demanded that the German navy cease its undersea raids on surface ships and for a time it did; but it then resumed the practice because the German high command calculated that submarine warfare was indispensable to the German war effort.[43] The resumption caused the United States to declare war on Germany on April 4, 1917. American trade policy thus indirectly and inadvertently catalyzed the country's entry into the European conflict.

In the wake of that war, having sent more than a million troops to France in 1917 and 1918 but then having declined to join the League of Nations, which Woodrow Wilson had helped to establish with the mission of maintaining the postwar peace, the United States sought to avoid taking part in the security affairs of Europe. America could not, however, or at least did not, avoid involvement in European economic matters, if only because of the loans it had made to Britain and France during the war that were still outstanding. In fact, the United States became entangled in a three-way economic relationship that proved to be both politically toxic and economically corrosive for Europe.

The postwar peace settlement imposed on Germany the obligation to pay reparations to Britain and France. The Germans regarded the requirement to do so as unfair and unjust; in the 1920s, they sometimes could not pay and at other times chose not to pay what they owed. The British and French not only felt morally and legally entitled to the reparations payments—they needed German funds to help service their American loans. Thus, in the 1920s, American banks loaned money to the Germans, who sent the money to the British and French, who handed it to the Americans, creating resentment as well as suboptimal economic performances in Europe.[44]

In these circumstances, the foreign economic policies of the United States proved counterproductive. Forgiving the British and French loans might have ended the politically and economically debilitating cycle of debts and payments in which the Europeans were locked; but the American government would not take steps to do so because, among other reasons, of public opposition to such an initiative.[45] In addition, the tariffs against imports that America maintained worsened Europe's economic conditions by inhibiting the Europeans' capacity to earn dollars to pay what they owed. Tariff reduction was not on the agenda of the Republican Party, which controlled the White House and the Congress in the decade following the war.[46] By aggravating Europe's economic problems, these American international economic policies also had political consequences. They had a negative impact on political relations among the European powers.

The United States did address the tangle of reparations and debts in a modest way through the Dawes Plan of 1924 and the Young Plan of 1929, both named for the American businessmen who took the lead in arranging them. Each reorganized the schedule of German reparations payments and provided for loans to Germany. The American government took no direct part in either—the loans came from private sources—but worked behind the scenes to encourage both.[47] The Plans brought some economic relief to Germany and had the related political effect of reducing, for a time, political acrimony on the Continent.

Then came the Great Depression, the steepest economic downturn of the industrial era.[48] American economic policy in response to the

Depression is notable, in retrospect, for what it did not do. The United States had the only economy large enough to take the lead in rescuing the world from the collapse.[49] American officials did not, however, envision such a role for their country. The administration of President Herbert Hoover, which was in office when the Depression struck, was committed to an economic orthodoxy that emphasized reduced government spending and high interest rates, which served only to make conditions worse. The Democrat Franklin D. Roosevelt, who assumed the presidency in 1933, ultimately abandoned that orthodoxy, but upon taking office declined to cooperate with the European countries to try to mitigate the effects of the Depression.[50]

As the most painful of those effects—massive unemployment—persisted in the early 1930s,[51] the world embarked on a path that would lead to the second great global conflict of the twentieth century. For the United States, that path went through Japan. Here again, as with World War I, the use of economic instruments produced an unintended and unwelcome political result, and it was the same result in both cases: despite its efforts to avoid the fighting, America found itself a full-fledged participant in the war.

Japan was the first non-Western country to harness the techniques of the Industrial Revolution, and as its economy became increasingly industrialized and ever larger, the country came to depend on the United States for raw materials not found in the Japanese archipelago.[52] Beginning in the 1930s, the Japanese–American economic relationship became hostage to Japan's foreign policy, which took, from Washington's perspective, an alarming turn. Japan moved to seize control of its giant but then very weak neighbor China, invading Manchuria in 1931 and then north China in 1937.

American leaders found Japan's campaign of political and economic expansion through military aggression geopolitically threatening and morally objectionable. Washington responded first by refusing to recognize the Japanese conquests and then by levying a series of economic sanctions on Japan. These included, among other measures, the cancellation of the 1911 economic treaty between the two countries and restrictions on the sale of aviation fuel and scrap metals.[53] The sanctions had as their goal deterring further Japanese aggression in Asia and ultimately compelling Japan to leave China. They achieved neither result. As often with economic sanctions, the Japanese deemed their East Asian policy sufficiently valuable to make it worth absorbing the costs that the American restrictions imposed on them rather than changing that policy.[54]

President Roosevelt sought to strike a balance in confronting Japan: making clear American opposition to that country's campaign of conquest and exacting an economic price for it but without triggering a Japanese–American war. He was increasingly worried about Hitler's comparable program of expansion in Europe and, if the United States became involved in the hostilities there, he did not want to have to fight on two fronts.[55]

In the summer of 1941, Japan pushed into southern Indochina, still technically a French possession although Germany had defeated France and occupied much of it in the spring and summer of 1940. In response, the American government included oil on the list of items the United States would not sell to Japan. Roosevelt had not intended to impose a complete ban on oil sales: he had been advised that oil was so important to Japan that Tokyo would regard a total denial as a cause of war.[56] The administrative guidelines for oil restrictions were, however, interpreted in such a way as to make the ban total; and Roosevelt was reluctant to be seen to be appeasing Japan by modifying the order, so he let it stand.[57]

The Japanese government proceeded to authorize, and the Japanese navy to carry out, a surprise attack on the American naval base at Pearl Harbor, Hawaii, on December 7, 1941. This provoked a congressional declaration of war on Japan. The use by the United States of an economic instrument of foreign policy thus contributed to an immensely consequential, if unsought, political outcome.

As Nazi Germany overturned one after another of the provisions of the post–World War I settlement in the 1930s, the United States did not impose economic sanctions in the way that it did in response to Japan's comparable course in Asia. When war broke out in Europe in 1939, America once again declared its neutrality; but while Woodrow Wilson had genuinely wished not to take sides in the First World War, Franklin Roosevelt had a different view in the Second. Roosevelt believed that a German victory would severely damage American interests. When, with the fall of France in June 1940, such a victory appeared imminent, the president became active in aiding the British, and, after the German attack on the Soviet Union of June 22, 1941, in assisting Soviet resistance to Germany as well.

In the 1930s, the American Congress had passed three "Neutrality Acts" to keep the United States at a distance from the conflict in Europe, but Roosevelt succeeded in both weakening and getting around them. He secured congressional authorization for two programs of military assistance: an exchange of American naval destroyers for British military bases in the Western hemisphere in 1940 and the Lend-Lease Act of 1941, under the terms of which Britain "borrowed" military equipment from the United States.[58]

Because both involved sending military assets across the Atlantic, neither qualifies as the use of a purely economic instrument for political goals. They do have a rough historical parallel with a strategy historically employed by Great Britain known as offshore balancing. In the eighteenth century in particular, but also before and afterward, the British government sent financial subventions to European powers opposing a state seeking domination of the Continent. British interests required an equilibrium of power among all the major countries rather than the hegemony of a single one, and British stipends helped the countries resisting a bid for domination purchase the troops they needed. London hoped that such assistance to European powers would obviate the need for Britain to send its own forces to the Continent for this purpose.[59] The American policy toward Europe between the fall of France and Pearl Harbor similarly aimed at preventing a single power—Nazi Germany—from dominating Europe without having to dispatch American troops there.

Ultimately, of course, American military personnel did fight in Europe and in Asia. The United States made a major military contribution to the outcome of World War II. The American economy also contributed to the Allied victory by producing a large share of the weapons used not only by American forces but also by those of America's principal allies, Great Britain and the Soviet Union. In the Second World War, America served as the "arsenal of democracy."[60] The historian Paul Kennedy has written that in major wars victory usually goes to the side with the larger economic base.[61] Thanks to the size and productivity of the American economy, in World War II that distinction belonged to the coalition opposing Nazi Germany and Imperial Japan.

THE COLD WAR, 1945–1990

In the wake of World War II, the winning coalition broke apart. Its two most powerful members, the United States and the Soviet Union, became rivals, and their rivalry, known as the Cold War, dominated global affairs until the last decade of the twentieth century. The war that ended in 1945 increased the margin of economic superiority the United States enjoyed over all other countries.[62] Because it had the only major industrial economy that had avoided substantial destruction in wartime, in the early postwar years the United States was responsible by some estimates for more than 40 percent of the world's total output, an unprecedented proportion for a single country.

At the outset of the Cold War and thereafter, the scale of its economic resources gave America an unmatched capacity for the use of economic instruments to pursue its political goals. It had a compelling incentive to use them: as it and other countries had regularly done, America deployed its economic resources to prosecute the conflict in which it was engaged, a conflict that unfolded over four and one-half decades. America's use of economic tools for political purposes during the Cold War differed from its previous use of them, however, in three ways.

First, economic tools became more important during the conflict with the Soviet Union because after 1945 military instruments were devalued. With the advent of nuclear weapons, the all-out wars that great powers had waged in the past, such as the two world wars, had become prohibitively expensive. Second, while before 1945 the United

States had deployed its economic instruments primarily to punish adversaries, during the Cold War it used trade and finance, frequently and on a large scale, for the purposes of recruiting and strengthening friends. Finally, the American economy mattered politically in the Cold War in a new way. The conflict was, among other things, a conflict of political and especially economic systems. The two sides organized economic life in radically different ways—the United States through free markets, the Soviet Union according to bureaucratic commands. Each sought to demonstrate that its own system of production was superior to—that is, more productive than—that of the other.‡ The outcome of the Cold War owed a great deal to the relative performances of the two economic systems.

Even before World War II had ended, the United States engaged in a seminal exercise in international economic policymaking, planning for the reconstruction and modification of the global rules and institutions governing cross-border finance and commerce.[63] In 1944, an international conference held at Bretton Woods, New Hampshire, drafted a plan for a new international monetary order to replace the nineteenth-century gold standard, which had all but expired during the Great Depression. What came to be known as the Bretton Woods system provided for greater flexibility in national monetary policy than the gold standard had permitted. It had the American dollar as its anchor, supplementing (and effectively replacing) gold. Bretton Woods had a significance beyond its specific results, as consequential as they were, in that it established a precedent for active and ongoing, rather than episodic, American involvement in international economic affairs. This

‡ "Comparisons between the two systems, and therefore competition between them in the promotion of economic welfare, thus became a major theme of the international history of the second half of the twentieth century. This competition was especially vivid because during that period several countries—Germany, Korea, China, and for a time Vietnam—were divided, with one part adopting free-market practices and the other employing central planning. These divided countries offered the closest approximation political life can provide of a controlled experiment to determine which system performed better. The results of that experiment had a great deal to do with how the Cold War ended." Michael Mandelbaum, *The Four Ages of American Foreign Policy: Weak Power, Great Power, Superpower, Hyperpower,* New York: Oxford University Press, 2022, p. 248.

became a foundational principle of the country's foreign policy during the Cold War and beyond. The United States also took the lead in establishing new global rules for cross-border trade, which were embodied in the General Agreement on Tariffs and Trade (GATT).

The American government, and the other governments that took part in designing the new trade and monetary regimes, had, first and foremost, economic motives for doing so. Experience had taught them that international economic activity requires rules for its optimal functioning; they were confident (rightly, as it turned out) that robust international trade, lending, and investment would enhance the economic well-being of the countries engaged in it. In addition, the memory of the Great Depression hovered over their deliberations, and they believed that what they were creating would help to prevent another such disastrous economic downturn. The participating governments, including the American one, also understood the Depression to have fostered the political conditions that produced World War II,[64] a repetition of which they also earnestly hoped to avoid. Thus, their economic rule–making and institution-building had a political as well as an economic aim.

In the wake of World War II, the United States and the world managed to avoid another Depression, but not another great-power conflict. The first tools of foreign policy that America deployed in waging that new conflict were economic ones.[65] In 1947, as a civil war raged in Greece between communist and anti-communist forces, the administration of President Harry Truman announced a program of assistance to Greece and also to Turkey. The president's speech to Congress proposing it functioned as the American declaration of the Cold War. "I believe," he said, "that it must be the policy of the United States to support free peoples who are resisting attempted subjugation by armed minorities or by outside pressures."[66]

To sustain resistance to communism in the two countries, the United States offered $400 million in military but also economic aid.[67] The commitment to provide such assistance to other countries facing similar threats came to be known as the Truman Doctrine. Its goal—preventing the spread of communism—became the principal American geopolitical aim for four decades, to which it devoted economic as well as political and military resources.

Also in 1947, the United States launched an even larger program of economic assistance, for the same general purpose. American officials became concerned that the continuing, war-imposed economic disorder in Western Europe[68] would serve as a breeding ground for popular sympathy for Soviet-style communism—France and Italy both had large Communist Parties—and for Soviet subversion of democratic governments there.[69] America therefore proceeded to transfer capital to the countries of Western Europe on an unprecedentedly large scale. Under the terms of what was formally called the European Recovery Program (ERP) but became better known as the Marshall Plan after Truman's secretary of state, George C. Marshall, who announced it, Europe received a total of $13 billion between 1948 and 1952, an enormous sum at that time.[70] The contrast with American policy toward Europe after 1918 was striking. In the wake of World War I, the United States refused to cancel Europe's debts: following World War II, the American government made generous grants to the war-battered countries of the western part of the Continent.[71]

Marshall Plan funds did help to ignite economic recovery in Europe, launching what would prove to be a remarkable run of growth that the French called *les trente glorieuses*—the thirty glorious years. Marshall aid also established a precedent for the American use of economic instruments—in this case financial ones—as incentives. By catalyzing economic growth, the Marshall Plan helped to achieve two major and related American political goals: consolidating democratic governance in Europe and strengthening the European recipients' ties to the United States.

American economic instruments, in the form of the Marshall Plan, had another momentous political effect. The Soviet Union did not participate in the program and prevented the countries of Central and Eastern Europe that the Red Army had occupied during the course of World War II, and upon which Moscow had already imposed or soon would impose communist governments, from accepting Marshall aid. The Plan thus made a major contribution to the descent of what Winston

Churchill called an "Iron Curtain" across the middle of Europe, dividing the Continent between a capitalist, democratic, pro-American West and a communist east dominated by the Soviet Union.[72]

A final political effect of Marshall aid turned out to be the longest-lasting, and perhaps ultimately the most significant, of all. The American government made economic cooperation among the countries of Western Europe a condition for receiving the grants it was offering.[73] The cooperation they practiced laid the basis for the process of economic integration in Europe that gave rise first to the European Common Market, then to the European Community, and finally to the European Union (EU). By 2024, the EU consisted of 27 members who traded freely among themselves. It allowed freedom of individual movement among its member countries, most of whom used a common currency.[74]

The postwar policy of the United States toward Japan resembled its approach to Europe. Immediately after the war, the American occupation authority, headed by General Douglas MacArthur, concentrated on transforming Japanese politics to make them more democratic. With the onset of the Cold War, however, the American emphasis shifted to promoting the revival of the Japanese economy. The greatest American contribution to that revival came when war broke out on the Korean peninsula in June 1950, and the United States made major purchases in Japan to support the war effort in Korea. This boosted Japanese economic growth.[75] The United States also provided the largest market for Japanese exports. In the three decades after World War II, thanks in part to direct and indirect American economic assistance, the Japanese economy followed the same sharply upward trajectory as the economies of Western Europe, and with the same political result: the country became solidly democratic and a reliable and increasingly wealthy American ally. Here again, an economic instrument of American foreign policy had a major, and in this case very much intended, political effect.

The Cold War use of economic instruments as incentives rather than sanctions in pursuit of political goals extended to trade as well as finance. Under the auspices of the GATT, the United States took the lead in organizing and bringing to successful conclusions eight multilateral tariff-lowering trade rounds between the late 1940s and the mid-1980s.[76] The success was made possible by a change in the domestic politics of trade policy in the United States, which led, over the decades, to a very substantial lowering of trade barriers around the world. This particular chapter of American international economic policy also had political as well as economic aims.[77]

The Great Depression, and the New Deal that the administration of Franklin D. Roosevelt enacted to counteract its effects, made the Democrats the majority political party in the United States for the first time since before the Civil War. Led by Roosevelt's Secretary of State Cordell Hull, a former congressman from Tennessee who was more passionately committed to free trade than any other senior American official in the twentieth century,[78] the Congress passed the Reciprocal Tariff Adjustment Act (RTAA) in 1934, which made it easier for the president to negotiate tariff reductions with other countries.[79]

The tariff reduction that the RTAA made possible gained momentum after 1945, for two reasons. First, the war had so devastated the rest of the world that the United States had an economic advantage in almost every tradeable product. The normal politics of trade, pitting the winners, who favored free trade, against the losers from cross-border commerce, who advocated protection, were suspended because virtually no sector of the American economy was a loser.[80] Second, the Cold War meant that the United States placed an exceptionally high political value on promoting the prosperity of actual and potential allies in the struggle against the Soviet Union. Expanding trade, that is, had the same political motive as the Marshall Plan,[81] and, as it turned out, the same result. Participants in international trade after 1945 did become wealthier, not least by virtue of access to the domestic American market, the largest in the world. As they prospered, they became, American officials believed, less vulnerable to Soviet assault from without and less susceptible to communist subversion from within.

By the 1960s, Western Europe no longer needed economic assistance from the United States and had, for the most part, solidly democratic, pro-American governments. The principal battleground of the Cold War, in American eyes, had shifted to poor countries outside Europe— many of them recently released from European imperial rule—that came to be known, collectively, as the Third World.[82] The American government adopted the approach to the Third World that had proven successful with Western Europe and Japan. It sought to promote economic growth through grants and loans, animated by the conviction that growth provided the antidote to the communist political advances that it continued to be the central aim of American foreign policy to resist. The United States understood the Cold War to be, as well as a military confrontation, a contest between two distinct economic systems, and believed that the one that better assisted the universal Third World pursuit of economic development would gain a major advantage in the overall competition.

In 1961, the administration of President John F. Kennedy established the Agency for International Development to preside over the disbursement of foreign aid to poor countries around the world. In the same year, it created the Alliance for Progress,[83] which worked exclusively with Latin America. The United States also made use of the resources of an institution founded in 1944 at Bretton Woods with a European focus, which had shifted its orientation to the Third World: the International Bank for Reconstruction and Development, commonly known as the World Bank.[84] The Bank's capital came from a number of donor countries but the United States exercised major influence over it; its president was always an American citizen. Foreign aid to the Third World, as the United States practiced it, may be seen as a version of the longer-standing American policy of state-building,[85] supplying one crucial ingredient—capital—to help poor countries build their own states.

Their accomplishments in attempting to do so varied widely. Foreign assistance beyond Europe had a more mixed record of success than did the Marshall Plan. Few if any of the recipient countries had the bases for sustained economic growth that Western Europe possessed even after the terrible damage and disruption of World War II: an industrial base, the well-developed institutions of a free-market system, an educated workforce, and an effectively functioning national government. In the last three decades of the Cold War, the countries of the Third World grew at widely varying rates, and many factors other than the scope of American generosity toward them determined how fast they managed to grow. The remarkable post-1979 growth of the People's Republic of China, for example, would not have been possible without China's access to the American market but had almost nothing to do with official foreign aid from the United States.

While employing trade- and finance-based incentives, the United States also resorted to a more familiar economic instrument—sanctions—in the conflict with the Soviet Union. America imposed sanctions directly on its principal adversary less frequently and less extensively than other countries at war in the past had often done because the communist nuclear superpower effectively sanctioned itself. That is, because of the central planning that dominated its economic life, it engaged in very little trade and investment with the market economies of the non-communist world,[86] so there was almost no commerce to terminate as a method of punishment.

There were a few exceptions to this pattern. Since the Cold War included an arms race in which the two sides sought to develop the most sophisticated and lethal weaponry, the American government established CoCom—the Coordinating Committee for Multilateral Export Controls—to prevent the leakage of America's most advanced militarily relevant technologies to the Soviet Union and its communist satellites. In addition, in response to the Soviet invasions of Afghanistan in 1979 and the Soviet-inspired crackdown by the communist government of Poland on the free trade union Solidarity in 1981, the American government levied a series of specific economic sanctions.[87]

When Fidel Castro seized power in Cuba in 1959 and declared himself a communist and an ally of the Soviet Union, the United States imposed broad economic sanctions that continued for decades,[88] outliving the Cold War itself. Successive American governments and the American public as a whole had a special sensitivity about the Caribbean island because of its location, a mere ninety miles from the coast of the United States. By virtue of its proximity, its relatively small population,[89] and its history of economic dependence on its giant neighbor to the north, Cuba was, in theory, particularly vulnerable to an American economic embargo. While the American-imposed sanctions caused great inconvenience to the communist government in Havana, and while the emigration of many of its most talented people further weakened it economically, the Castro regime survived, in no small part because the Soviet Union gave it economic support.

American economic sanctions during the Cold War were perhaps most effective not when applied to adversaries but on those rare occasions when Washington imposed them on friendly countries.[90] When Great Britain, in concert with France and Israel, seized the Suez Canal in the fall of 1956, the British sought loans to shore up their national financial position. Disapproving of the seizure, the United States blocked the loans until the British government agreed to withdraw from Suez.[91]

In the final decades of the Cold War, America levied sanctions against countries for political purposes that had little or nothing to do with the global rivalry with the Soviet Union.[92] Notably, it penalized South Africa for its policy of racial apartheid, which ended in the early 1990s. It also used economic sanctions in an attempt to prevent communist North Korea and non-communist but hostile Iran from building their own nuclear weapons, efforts that, like the sanctions against Cuba, continued after the Cold War ended.

In general, therefore, during the Cold War the United States offered economic incentives to actual and potential allies and directed economic sanctions at adversaries, in conformity with the age-old geopolitical norm of rewarding friends and punishing foes. On one occasion, however, the American government mixed the two approaches, making access to the American market and American capital available to an adversary—indeed, to its primary Cold War adversary, the Soviet Union.

The Nixon administration's early-1970s policy of détente with Moscow included an initiative that came to be called "linkage." The initiative rested on the belief—or the hope—that Soviet economic engagement with the United States would entangle the communist superpower in a web of interdependence that would restrain it from taking political steps harmful to the security of America and its allies. Soviet good conduct, that is, would be linked to economic benefits from the West.[93]

Linkage did not achieve its aim. The two countries turned out to have incompatible understandings of what détente involved, and Moscow did not abandon policies unacceptable to America and the West. Moreover, because distrust of the Soviet Union remained a powerful current in American political life, the proposed program of economic cooperation proved abortive. The Nixon administration had promised Moscow Most Favored Nation trading status, but Congress blocked it through the Jackson–Vanik amendment, which required Moscow to permit free emigration in order to receive it, something that the Soviet authorities refused to do.[94]

The Cold War concluded on terms highly favorable to the United States and the West, with the liberation of the countries of Eastern Europe from communist rule and the breakup of the Soviet Union. Economic considerations had a major bearing on this outcome, although not through the explicit American use of economic instruments of foreign policy.

While the United States and the West experienced economic difficulties in the 1970s,[95] by the middle of the 1980s the result of the Cold War contest of economic systems[96] had become clear: the free-market economies of the West had decisively outperformed the centrally planned systems of the communist world.[97] Western economic superiority weakened the appeal of communism around the world, deflated the confidence of the people living in communist countries in the way that they were being governed,[98] and aroused concern among Soviet leaders that their capitalist adversaries would turn their economic success into a dangerous military advantage.

A new leader, Mikhail Gorbachev, came to power in Moscow in 1985 determined to accelerate Soviet economic growth in order to restore the appeal of communism and preserve the country's status as a military superpower.[99] To this end, he instituted a series of economic and political reforms, including declining to intervene militarily to keep communist leaders in power in Eastern Europe as Soviet leaders had done in the past. The Gorbachev reforms led, over the course of six turbulent years and entirely unintentionally, to the collapse of the Soviet Union, the disappearance of communism in Europe and, by virtue of these epochal developments, the end of the conflict that had dominated America's relations with the world for most of the second half of the twentieth century.

Its end ushered in a new era in European and world history, and therefore in the history of American foreign policy—one in which, albeit in some new ways, the United States continued to deploy economic tools in pursuit of political aims.

THE POST–COLD WAR ERA AND AFTER

The end of the Cold War left the United States in a position of unprecedented global power. In military terms, America towered over all other countries. While a smaller proportion of global output came from America than had been the case at the end of World War II, the free-market system had triumphed around the world and virtually every country that lacked one rushed to adopt it. In these circumstances, the American government had little need to levy economic sanctions against the country's adversaries: for the moment, at least, it had—or seemed to have—no major adversaries. The sanctions that it did impose often had political goals other than defending the United States against a serious threat, although some did have that purpose. As for economic incentives, in the wake of the Cold War, America continued to rely on them to achieve political goals. In fact, they became central to an informal doctrine that came to stand at the heart of American foreign policy.

As the new era began, the United States was penalizing China economically. In 1989, the regime had cracked down brutally on demonstrators in Beijing and other cities. The Clinton administration, which took office in 1993, decided that China would not receive the trade privileges with America to which it had become accustomed unless it did more to respect the rights of Chinese citizens.[100] The Chinese government did not change its practices on human rights, and Clinton soon abandoned the effort to compel it to do so.[101]

Throughout the post–Cold War era, the United States, joined by many other countries, continued the economic sanctions on North Korea and Iran[102] that were intended to persuade the autocratic governments of both countries to abandon their nuclear-weapons programs.

Here, sanctions were deployed for the familiar purpose of counteracting threats. Neither effort, however, succeeded,[103] and North Korea did build and test such weapons. China contributed to the failure of the sanctions on North Korea by keeping open its border with that country and allowing food and fuel, which the North Korean regime could not readily obtain elsewhere, to pass across it.

With Iran, American presidents consistently declared that they would not allow the regime that held power there to acquire nuclear armaments, implying that the United States would use military force to prevent this; but through 2024 the American government had not made the threat to attack the Iranian nuclear facilities sufficiently credible to the ruling clerics to divert them from their nuclear goal. In June 2025, the United States did bomb Iranian nuclear-weapons facilities, although the Iranian government apparently did not, as a result, give up its nuclear-weapons program. In both cases, sanctions failed for a familiar reason. The goal that the sanctions were designed to persuade the target countries to abandon was sufficiently valuable to the rulers (the public had no say in the matter in either country) that they were willing to pay a very high economic price to continue to pursue it.

Incentives as well as sanctions played a role in American foreign policy in the post–Cold War period. A series of financial crises in the 1990s afforded an opportunity to use the provision of capital for political purposes. Most of the stricken countries applied to the International Monetary Fund, in which America exercised substantial influence, for emergency loans. (In Mexico's financial crisis, that country relied largely on the United States.)[104] The loans came with economic conditions, but sometimes had the effect of promoting political change as well. In Indonesia, the long-serving dictator left power and an elected government eventually replaced him.[105]

America assigned a far more ambitious post–Cold War political role to the lure of access to American and Western trade and finance. That access formed a crucial part of a linked series of ideas about the relationship between politics and economics that, while never codified in a formal doctrine, pervaded American foreign policy after the Cold War ended. Not simply out of faith, but on the basis of the history that they themselves had witnessed, American policymakers assumed these ideas to be true. These officials did act on these ideas, although they did not always feel the need to say explicitly that that was what they were doing.

A series of interconnected propositions, each of which seemed to be strongly supported by the events and trends of recent history, comprised what might be called the liberal theory of history.[106] The first proposition asserted that prosperity had become a universal goal; and, indeed, vanishingly few were the governments that did not seriously aspire to economic growth, at least in order to enhance their own countries' national power if not always to increase the individual well-being of the population. The key to prosperity, the next proposition held, lies in having a free-market economy and engaging in commerce with the rest of the world. The outcome of the Cold War, coupled with China's surging growth after turning part of its economy over to markets, seemed to have validated that proposition; and virtually all of the formerly communist countries discarded central planning as the governing principle of economic organization and tried, with varying degrees of success, to install the institutions of the free market.

Those two propositions led to a third, for which compelling evidence also seemed to be available. Active participation in free markets, and a rising level of prosperity, tended to propel countries in a democratic political direction.[107] Finally, according to the fourth tenet of the liberal theory of history, engaging in commerce and practicing democracy conduce to peace. The example of the EU, above all, testified to the validity of this proposition. Ever-closer economic integration and the democratic political systems of the member countries had turned the European continent, for centuries a breeding ground of warfare, into an island of peace. These four propositions formed the basis for the Clinton administration's proclamation of its international goal as the "enlargement" of the global community of peaceful democracies.[108]

The components of this post–Cold War American worldview had pre-twentieth century intellectual and political antecedents. The founders of the United States had faith that the political system they established had peace-inducing properties.[109] The conviction that commerce has pacifying effects goes back to the eighteenth-century French writer

Montesquieu and was taken up by prominent political figures in Great Britain in the mid-nineteenth century as part of a campaign in favor of free trade.[110] In his 1795 essay *Perpetual Peace*, the German philosopher Immanuel Kant argued that republican governments were less likely to go to war than autocratic ones, and professional students of politics in the twentieth century found supporting evidence in the history, especially the recent history, of international relations.[111]

While the individual propositions were not new, the liberal theory of history represented an innovation because it brought them together and because, for the first time, historical developments seem to bear them out. The course of global history, Americans found reason to believe during the last decade of the twentieth century, had brought the world to the point at which the political and economic principles the United States favored reinforced each other, and the combination of them was making the world a more peaceful, prosperous, and democratic place than ever before. The countries of the EU largely shared this American outlook.

Economic incentives played a central part in the liberal theory of history, and the United States sought to provide these when they seemed likely to contribute to democracy and peace. The Clinton administration furnished economic assistance to Russia's fledgling, fragile, post-Soviet experiment in democracy.[112] It lifted the sanctions it had imposed on China—partly, to be sure, in response to political pressure from the American business community, with its eye on lucrative opportunities for trade there, but also based on the belief that, as it became increasingly integrated into the international economy, China's politics, including its government's approach to human rights, would move in a democratic direction.[113]

In the wake of the Cold War, more and more countries came to participate more and more extensively in international trade and investment. The term "globalization" denoted this trend, and the United States adopted policies to promote it. Washington signed a series of bilateral trade accords,[114] entered into the North American Free Trade Agreement with Canada and Mexico,[115] and helped to conclude the Uruguay Round of multilateral trade negotiations.[116] The United States also took part in establishing an international body to govern and facilitate cross-border commerce, the International Trade Organization, and then sponsored Chinese membership in it.

Globalization was the linchpin of the liberal theory of history, and its promotion constituted the most prominent and ambitious American use of economic instruments for political purposes in the post–Cold War period. The rapid and large-scale economic integration of the 1990s, however, generated a backlash. In the countries of the Third World—a term less frequently used after the Cold War—the financial crises caused by increased inflows of funds from abroad dampened enthusiasm for receiving foreign capital. Nor were financial difficulties confined to the poor countries. The global financial crisis of 2008, triggered by the United States, and the subsequent difficulties of the EU's common currency, the euro, brought home to all countries the hazards of large-scale cross-border capital flows.[117]

In the wealthy countries, especially the United States, increased trade produced, as it inevitably does, losers as well as winners. The losers took to the political arena to advocate protection from the foreign products that competed with and displaced what the industries in which they worked made. The opposition culminated in 2016, with both major presidential candidates rejecting the carefully negotiated free trade agreement with Asia called the Trans-Pacific Partnership. That year saw the election to the presidency of a candidate, Donald Trump, who opposed free trade more emphatically than any American chief executive in almost a century.[118]

The rejection of expanded trade crippled one of America's principal economic tools for pursuing political goals. At the same time, the political trajectories of China and Russia put an end to the hope that globalization would lead to enduring international peace. Contrary to the liberal theory of history, despite participating in the global economy, neither country became a democracy and both came to adopt aggressive foreign policies. These foreign policies drove the United States back to the economic instrument familiar from American history: sanctions.

Over its nearly four decades of rapid economic growth, China did become a less repressive, more open country than it had been under Mao

Zedong, who presided over the ruling Communist Party from 1949 to 1976; and in that time the People's Republic pursued a relatively peaceful foreign policy. These developments almost certainly had something to do with the country's transition to a partially market-based economy and the trade with and investment from the West during the post-Mao period. To the extent that they did, they vindicated, at least up to a point, the liberal theory of history.[119]

Then, however, Xi Jinping, who became the supreme Chinese leader in 2011, took the country in a different direction. He imposed greater repression at home and carried out an increasingly aggressive policy toward China's neighbors. As a result, during his first decade in power, the predominant image of China in the United States changed. Where once Americans had seen it as following a path toward democracy and peace, they increasingly came to perceive what was still, in political terms, a communist country as a major threat to America, its allies in Asia, and its global interests.

China's rapid progress in mastering digital technology alarmed American policymakers. It held out the prospect that Chinese firms, with close ties to the communist government, would be able to install digital infrastructure around the world, including in the West. This, the American government feared, would give the communist authorities in Beijing unprecedented and dangerous access to, and leverage over, the citizens and even the governments of the West. The United States therefore proceeded to take steps against the biggest and most aggressive Chinese telecommunications firm, Huawei, steps that succeeded in keeping it largely out of Western markets.[120]

China's technological progress also seemed, ominously, to portend the development of weaponry on a par with, or even more sophisticated than, that of the United States. Accordingly, the American government enacted legislation to block Chinese access to the products on the cutting edge of technology—the most advanced microchips. These came primarily from the West and from the democratically governed island of Taiwan off the Chinese coast and were becoming increasingly important for geopolitical competition and warfare.[121] The legislation had the same purpose as CoCom, the Cold War organization established to keep the most sophisticated militarily relevant technology of that era away from the Soviet Union. To achieve what had become the principal American political goal where China was concerned, containment of its power, economic sanctions replaced economic incentives.[122]

American policy toward Russia followed a comparable pattern. Since the breakup of the Soviet Union left Russia with only half the population the Communist multinational state had had, and because the post-Soviet Russian economy was smaller than the Soviet one had been and hardly a model of dynamic growth, twenty-first-century Russia posed a less formidable military challenge than did China. Under its own dictator, Vladimir Putin, however, Russia engaged in a more overtly aggressive policy toward its neighbors, which led to a full-scale invasion of Ukraine on February 24, 2022. In response, the United States and its European allies sent arms to the Ukraine to resist the Russian invaders and put in place economic sanctions of unprecedentedly broad scope.[123]

Those sanctions notably included financial ones, which the United States and its European allies were able to impose by making use of a new economic instrument, one that Washington had begun to wield two decades earlier. Just as goods have always moved across oceans, making it possible for powerful navies to interdict them, so in the twenty-first century finance—money—moved around the world via signals sent through fiber-optic cables that crisscrossed the planet. Almost all the cables passed, at some point, through the United States, giving the American government access to them. That fact, combined with the enormous importance of American financial institutions and the American financial market for the world economy, made it possible for the United States to find and suppress sources of funding for terrorism after the terrorist attacks on New York and Washington, DC, of September 11, 2001, and to bar the Islamic Republic of Iran from the global financial system in response to its ongoing nuclear-weapons program.[124]

After the Russian assault of February 24, 2022, by the use of this and other economic instruments against Moscow, trade and investment from the West came to a halt, disrupting supply chains on which Russia depended and depriving Putin's regime of some needed technologies. Key Russian financial institutions were sanctioned and cut off from the global financial system. Foreign firms operating in Russia left the country. Russian assets held outside Russia, including the reserves of its central bank, were frozen. Individuals associated with the regime, including wealthy Russians living in the West, became the targets of economic penalties. Europe took steps to lessen its dependence on Russian energy, with the aim of reducing the revenues the Russian regime derived from its sale.[125] This economic program aimed to erode the Russian government's capacity to wage war, the same goal that Great Britain had had, for example, in blockading Germany during World War I, and indeed the same goal that economic embargoes during wartime have had for centuries.

The Russian invasion of Ukraine, along with the increasingly hostile conduct of China in its region and beyond, made it clear that the period of global tranquility that had begun with the collapse of European communism and the conclusion of the Cold War had come to an end. The new post-post–Cold War era of American foreign policy that followed differed from the preceding one, with serious conflict having become a more prominent feature of international relations. It did, however, promise to have one feature in common with the post–Cold War era, and indeed with the entire history of American foreign policy going back to the eighteenth century. As in the past, the United States would use economic instruments—sanctions against China and Russia but also, perhaps, in dealing with other countries, access to trade and capital—in pursuit of its national political goals outside its own borders.

A Democratic Foreign Policy

DEMOCRACY AND FOREIGN POLICY

"We the people of the United States," the opening words of the preamble to the American Constitution of 1788, prefigure the third distinctive and enduring feature of America's relations with other countries: the United States has conducted an unusually democratic foreign policy. That is, in comparison with other countries, the people have had more influence on devising and carrying out the policies governing America's external relations. Embedded in the Constitution's beginning is its basic premise: that the people have the right to decide questions of public policy. To a great extent they have decided such questions, including in foreign policy.

By contrast, in the great powers of Europe at the time of America's founding, and for more than a century thereafter—indeed in most sovereign states for most of history—foreign policy was the preserve of the leader, not the people.[1] Unlike their counterparts in other countries, the people of the United States have participated extensively in, and had considerable influence on, the making of American foreign policy.

To be sure, as with the other two features that have made it distinctively American, the foreign policy of the United States has not always and for every issue had a singularly democratic character. On some occasions, in some ways, it has resembled the foreign policies of the rest of the world. Just as America has pursued realist as well as ideological goals abroad,[2] and just as it has used political and military instruments for economic purposes, as well as economic instruments for political and military purposes,[3] so it has sometimes followed the pattern of centralized, top-down, government-initiated, and government-controlled foreign policy familiar in most sovereign states for most of history. In the process of foreign policymaking, as with the goals of foreign policy, the difference between the United States and the rest of the world has been one of degree.

In the making of foreign policy in all countries, including the United States, executive authority enjoys particular advantages—access to information and the capacity to act swiftly and decisively among them. For that reason, in the conduct of foreign policy everywhere power tends to be concentrated.[4] Moreover, the 1788 Constitution reserves certain powers in foreign policy to the executive branch of the federal government. Notably, it makes the president what the principal leader in almost all countries has almost always been: the commander-in-chief of the armed forces. In the course of American history, in undertaking major foreign policies, including war, the president has sometimes acted in advance of, or even without, popular consent as expressed through the public's elected representatives in the Congress.

This tendency became particularly pronounced during the Cold War era. Near the beginning of that period, in June 1950, President Harry Truman broke with national tradition and constitutional requirement by dispatching troops to fight in Korea without obtaining authorization from Congress.[5] Presidential domination of foreign policy in that era went so far as to give rise to the assertion, by a noted political scientist, that America had, in effect, two distinct presidencies, with different powers—one for foreign and the other for domestic affairs.[6] In the same spirit, a well-known historian wrote a book with the thesis that the concentration of power over foreign policy in the hands of the chief executive had created an "imperial presidency."[7] In fact, the tradition of presidential control of foreign policy at the expense of popular influence predates the Cold War. It was in evidence, for example, in the Mexican War of 1846–1848, which President James K. Polk took the initiative in starting.[8]

After the Cold War, however, congressional votes on war became more frequent.[9] Moreover, in the course of American history, presidents have not wielded undiluted, unchallenged power in foreign policy. The Constitution includes provisions for a more democratic system of foreign policymaking than in other countries. It gives Congress the power to declare war and stipulates that international treaties must win the votes of two-thirds of the Senate to enter into force. In addition, cabinet officers, including those responsible for the nation's foreign relations, must receive the approval of a majority of the Senate in order to take office. The Constitution was written for the purpose, among others, of giving the infant United States a stronger government than its original governing document, the Articles of Confederation, had provided; but compared with the other governments of the world, the American one was, after 1788, less mighty, including in the conduct of foreign affairs.

The relatively democratic character of American foreign policy, starting at the founding of the republic, has a single, simple, straightforward cause: from the beginning, *all* American policies were subject to a greater degree of democratic influence than in other countries because its founders gave the United States a far more democratic political system than prevailed in the monarchies and empires of Europe and the rest in the world. Great Britain did have a government with a significant parliament, but the British monarch and the country's hereditary aristocracy exercised dominant influence over public policy, and especially over foreign policy. The United States, of course, had neither a monarch nor an aristocracy, which left far more scope for popular influence. Moreover, three specific features of America's representative democracy have made its process of foreign policymaking exceptionally democratic.

First, the principle of separation of powers that the Constitution enshrines creates multiple centers of political authority, and thus multiple channels through which the public can transmit its preferences in matters of policy, including foreign policy. The legislative as well as the executive branch has a role in the conduct of foreign affairs; and in the twentieth century the executive branch underwent a massive expansion, with its various departments—State, Defense, and the

Treasury especially—becoming not only far larger than previously* but also, because of their size, effectively more independent. By creating more centers of authority to which the public could appeal, this expanded the range of opportunities for the people to shape their country's external relations.[10]

The American people have been able to express their views on foreign policy and to press for their adoption because of a second feature of the American political system. The First Amendment of the 1788 Constitution guarantees freedom of speech as well as "the right of people peaceably to assemble and to petition the government for a redress of grievances." Americans have taken full advantage of these rights. The public has expressed its political views unceasingly since the first European settlers arrived in North America, and from the time of the Constitution's adoption a great deal of petitioning has taken place, some of it conveying the wishes of the public—or, more frequently, parts of the public—on matters of foreign policy.

The preferences thus expressed have affected public policy because of a third feature of the American system, which is the most important basis for the democratic character of the nation's foreign policy. This feature is, in fact, the central institution of American democracy: free, fair, and regular elections. In these elections, public officials pursuing policies not in harmony with public preferences can be, and regularly are, replaced. Elections are the ultimate instrument of democratic control of public policy, including foreign policy. Elected officials tend to be responsive to the wishes of the people because their jobs depend on their responsiveness.

Of the three distinctive features of American foreign policy—ideology, economics, and democracy—the third differs from the first two in an important way. Historically, the United States conducted an increasingly ideological foreign policy over time as it became more

---

* In 1802, "[a]side from 6,500 military personal, the federal bureaucracy nationwide amounted to 2,875 people, and the only way it affected the lives of the vast majority of Americans was by delivering mail." Walter A. McDougall, *Freedom Just Around the Corner: A New American History 1585–1828*, New York: HarperCollins, 2004, p. 374. By the third decade of the twenty-first century, the estimated total of federal employees was around two million.

powerful. The pursuit of ideological goals was most prominent in the last decade of the twentieth century and the first decade of the twenty-first, when the nation's relative power in the world reached its zenith. Similarly, the use of economic instruments for political goals accelerated with the expansion of the American economy. Not until the twentieth century, for example, did the government deploy capital for international political purposes.

By contrast, the United States had an exceptionally democratic approach to the making of foreign policy from the beginning. This did not change from the eighteenth century to the twenty-first. The rest of the present chapter therefore does not follow the same design as its two predecessors. It proceeds not chronologically but rather thematically. It is divided according to the principal mechanisms, from the smaller to the larger, by which the American people have brought their views to bear on the nation's international activities.

First to be considered are interest groups, which consist of people with common goals for public policy who organize themselves to try to persuade the government to adopt these goals. Next come political parties, larger organizations that, in the American context, encompass many interests and play a major role in the country's public life, including in its relations with other countries. Finally, this chapter considers public opinion—that is, the sentiments of the public as a whole. There is, of course, overlap among the three, and in general the larger the group seeking to affect public policy, the more successful its efforts are likely to be. James Madison, the fourth American president, deemed public opinion "the real sovereign" in a democracy,[11] and the history of the republic he helped to found bears this out.

Public opinion has had a major impact, down through the decades, on American foreign policy in general and in particular on the most important foreign policy of all: war.[12] The discussion of public opinion is divided into two sections because it has had two different and opposite effects on the nation's military policy: it has sometimes encouraged the United States to wage war, but at other times has worked against the resort to armed conflict, even when American troops were already in battle.

INTEREST GROUPS

From colonial days, Americans have had different ideas about politics and government, different ways of earning a living, different political and cultural affinities, and therefore different political and economic interests. Under the aegis of the First Amendment, they have organized to press for public policies that reflected and supported their interests. Indeed, one popular view of the American political system sees it as a forum for the interplay of many such groups, with public policy the outcome of that interplay.[13]

Such groups are composed of only tiny fractions of the overall American population and must operate in a political system in which majority rule is a governing principle; but American democracy affords the possibility for these groups to achieve their objectives, using the political channels that the American political system provides, even when they do not represent the majority. This typically occurs when two closely related conditions exist. The intensity of preferences on a particular issue inevitably varies across the society. It is often the case that some people, who feel that they have a major stake in the outcome of a particular issue and organize to promote their perspective, care far more about it than those who, while more numerous, have different, even opposing, preferences. Intensity, the first condition, can win the day when an issue has low salience among the public, which is the second. That is, an intense minority can prevail over the majority for whom the issue in question, whatever their views on it, has far less importance.

The classic instance of such a political dynamic is tariff policy. Any tax on imports, as the British economist David Ricardo demonstrated in the early nineteenth century, makes the country imposing it poorer overall. The benefits of imports, however, are diffused throughout the entire society and are so small—a price on the imported good slightly lower than it would be for one domestically produced—that the individuals receiving the benefit are not even aware that they are gaining something. By contrast, those injured by imports—for example, workers who become unemployed as a result of trade because imported goods drive their employers out of business—lose a great deal and are all too aware of their loss. When imports are permitted, the total gains exceed the total losses to a country, but the losers have a strong incentive to organize and press for tariff protection. The winners have virtually no incentive to push back to preserve their small, usually unnoticed gains. Every tariff is therefore an instance of high intensity combined with low salience carrying the day for a tiny minority.[†]

In foreign policy, interest groups, while not of negligible importance, have generally exerted less influence than they have on domestic matters. This is so because foreign policies often have much higher salience than domestic issues do. Foreign policies are carried out in the name, and on behalf, of the entire country. They involve matters of national security—not only the waging of wars (the most salient foreign-policy issue of all) but also diplomacy linked to the American position in the world. This has meant that groups focused on foreign policy have had the greatest success in persuading the government to act as they wish when their preferences have aligned with the sentiments of the American majority, and when the interest groups have advocated a direction that the nation was likely to take, or was already taking, for other reasons. For example, the United States has generally supported Israel because the American public, for a variety of reasons, has generally supported Israel.[14] In general, while interest groups have sought to affect foreign as well as domestic policy, and while they have sometimes had the satisfaction of seeing the government follow the course they have urged, their independent influence on foreign policy has almost always been modest and has often been overrated.

On occasion, foreign governments have acted as interest groups, trying to steer the foreign policy of the United States in directions beneficial

---

[†] Other economic issues follow this pattern. They typically concern "the allocation of resources on what qualifies—although they can involve billions of dollars—as a small scale: subsidies for one economic interest or another, for example, or the provisions of the tax code that affect a small number of the 320 million Americans. Relatively few people care (or even know) about these issues, and some of the few who do care can often get their way, modest though their numbers are. Minorities rather than majorities rule here in the sense that the vast majority of the public is disengaged, and a well-organized, highly motivated, and often well-financed minority can get its preferences adopted by the executive branch, or enacted into law by the Congress, or both." Michael Mandelbaum, *Mission Failure: America and the World in the Post–Cold War Era*, New York: Oxford University Press, 2016, pp. 17–18.

to them. The first envoy of revolutionary France, Edmond Charles Genet, attempted, upon his arrival in 1793, to enlist the American government in the French cause in its war with the European coalition opposing it. The French Revolution had friends in the United States, notably the first secretary of state and then third president Thomas Jefferson and his political associates, who at first responded favorably to Genet's schemes. Ultimately, however, the administration of George Washington, which adopted a policy of staying out of the European war, rebuffed the Frenchman.[15]

In the first century of America's existence as an independent country, the French effort proved to be unusual. This was so because, among other reasons, the United States was a weak power whose support the great powers of Europe did not find it worth exerting themselves to obtain. By the twentieth century, however, America had ceased to be weak. In the two world wars, Great Britain went to great lengths to win that support. It conducted a propaganda campaign during the first two years of World War I, the high point of which was the interception, decryption, and publication in January 1917, while the United States was still maintaining a formal policy of neutrality in the war, of the "Zimmermann Telegram." This was a secret message from the foreign minister of Germany, Britain's adversary, to his Mexican counterpart promising to return the territory the United States had taken from Mexico in the nineteenth century if, in the event that America entered the war as part of the anti-German coalition, Mexico sided with the Germans. The message did not go down well with Americans, which reinforced their sympathy for Britain and France.[16]

As in World War I, for the first two years of World War II the British tried to persuade the United States, once again formally neutral, to join it in opposing Germany.[17] As in the previous war, the United States eventually entered the fighting on Great Britain's side. As in World War I, American participation in the Second World War proved to be indispensable for the Allied victory.

Still, the course of the American policy during both wars demonstrates that Great Britain's efforts to move the United States did not alone persuade America to join either conflict. Pro-British sentiment before

America entered World War I arose in no small part from the extensive economic ties between the two countries, from which the United States greatly benefited. Moreover, it was Germany's campaign of unrestricted submarine warfare, not good will for Britain, that ultimately caused America to enter the war.

As for World War II, the American president of the day, Franklin D. Roosevelt, unlike his World War I era predecessor, Woodrow Wilson, strongly favored the British cause. He did not have to be persuaded by the British that their victory would be good, and a German triumph bad, for the United States. He did all he could to provide military assistance to Great Britain before formal American entry into the war. Nor did the American public have to be persuaded to sympathize with the British. However, it was not their sympathies but rather the Japanese attack on the American naval base at Pearl Harbor, Hawaii, on December 7, 1941, and the German leader Adolf Hitler's declaration of war on the United States four days later, that propelled American forces into active combat.

Unlike the French and British efforts, most interest groups active in American public affairs have consisted almost exclusively of Americans. The term commonly used for groups with both domestic and international concerns is "lobby,"[18] and the word does double duty: as a noun that refers to such groups and as a verb to describe their efforts to induce public officials to adopt their preferred policies.

During the Cold War, two lobbies in particular earned reputations for political potency, but turned out, in the end, to be less powerful than their reputations suggested. They thereby illustrated, as did the British campaigns to bring the United States into the two world wars, the limits to the sway that interest groups have held over American foreign policy.

The China lobby existed to further the interests of Chiang Kai-shek's government on the island of Taiwan, one hundred miles from the southeast coast of China.[19] Chiang and his Kuomintang party had lost the Chinese Civil War to Mao Zedong's communists and had repaired to the island, still claiming to be the legitimate government of the mainland. This lobby had its origins during World War II, when it sought to generate support for Chiang's China against the invading Japanese, and after the retreat to Taiwan it worked to forestall official American diplomatic recognition of the Communist regime in Beijing and its admission to the United Nations.

For the first part of the Cold War, the United States regarded the government of the mainland—the People's Republic of China—as an integral part of the global communist movement that it was America's central international purpose to oppose. In political terms, therefore, the China lobby was pushing against an open door. In 1972, however, when President Richard Nixon decided that a rapprochement with Mao's China would confer substantial strategic advantages on the United States, his administration effected such a rapprochement, and in dramatic fashion, with a presidential visit to Beijing. The China lobby was unable to prevent it.

Another Cold War interest group that gained a reputation for effectiveness in swaying the federal government, particularly its financial expenditures, was what Dwight Eisenhower, in his farewell address as president, called the "military-industrial complex." By that term he meant the nexus of the country's large armed forces and the defense industries that produced the increasingly complicated, sophisticated, and expensive armaments that these forces deployed. He warned that this complex might acquire "unwarranted influence" over the nation's allocation of resources as well as its foreign policy more generally.[20] Eisenhower spoke of what might happen, but many came to believe that the military-industrial complex did have an outsize role in budgetary and military matters.[21]

During the Cold War, the United States did indeed field large peacetime armed forces for the first time in its history and did see the emergence, also for the first time, of large manufacturing enterprises that depended for their profits and therefore for their existence on the production of weaponry. These institutions were necessary to sustain the extended competition with the Soviet Union that followed World War II. When that competition ended at the outset of the 1990s, however, the proportion of American economic output devoted to military purposes fell by half. In the absence of a pressing foreign threat, the military-industrial complex, such as it was, could not preserve its economic position.

The most enduring American foreign-policy lobbies arise from the immigration that has populated the nation from the beginning. It has given the United States diasporas—groups of people from the same country who retain connections to, or at least sympathies for, their own and their forebears' countries of origin. Such people have often acquired a social identity known as ethnicity, combining fidelity to the United States with continuing affinities for the old country.[‡] Ethnic groups have organized themselves to promote their original countries' interests in the foreign policy of the increasingly powerful country to which they have moved. Immigration on a large scale took place in the nineteenth century, particularly its second half, but because a generation or two usually passes before the immigrants and their children feel sufficiently settled to participate in American public life, ethnic lobbies did not become a significant part of American foreign policy until the twentieth century.

Two ethnic groups that arrived in the nineteenth century, the Germans and the Irish, were active in advance of American entry into the two world wars, seeking to prevent it on both occasions.[22] Both groups regarded American participation in a British-led coalition, which is the course that the United States eventually followed in both conflicts, to be injurious to the interests of their former homelands. This was certainly true for Germany, against which the United States fought in both wars. Irish Americans opposed what ultimately became American policy in the two conflicts because they saw Britain as Ireland's imperial oppressor. Before the First World War, Ireland was in fact a British possession, but opposition to American intervention in Europe persisted afterward, in advance of World War II, when an independent Irish republic had come into existence (while the six northeastern counties of the island

[‡] Nathan Glazer and Daniel P. Moynihan, Beyond the Melting Pot: The Negroes, Puerto Ricans, Jews, *Italians and Irish of New York City*, Second Edition, Cambridge, Massachusetts: M.I.T. Press, 1970, pp. xxxiii–xxxiv. "[D]iasporas may be compared to a bride in some traditional societies. She moves voluntarily from the home in which she has been raised to that of her new husband. She retains ties with and obligations to her original family, which are well established in custom. But these are not supposed to conflict with her duties to her new family, to which she owes her primary obligations." Michael Mandelbaum, "Introduction," in Michael Mandelbaum, editor, *The New European Diasporas: National Minorities and Conflict in Eastern Europe*, New York: The Council on Foreign Relations, 2000, p. 2.

remained part of the United Kingdom). On both occasions, the march of events—German submarine warfare and the Japanese attack on Pearl Harbor—overrode the wishes of German and Irish Americans.

Poles arrived in the United States later than did Germans and Irish. By the end of World War II, though, they had become politically important enough that, at his February 1945 summit meeting at Yalta on the Black Sea with the Soviet leader Josef Stalin (as well as the British prime minister Winston Churchill), President Franklin D. Roosevelt appealed to Stalin for fair treatment of Poland, which the Red Army had occupied in its campaign against Nazi Germany. While the importance of Polish American votes in American elections persuaded the American president to espouse Poland's cause, however, it did not move Stalin. For him, Polish votes in the United States, or indeed anywhere else, had no significance. Neither Roosevelt nor his successor, Harry Truman, managed to prevent Moscow from imposing a communist government on Poland.

The United States did support, although largely rhetorically, the Polish people's efforts to resist their communist overlords in the decades after the war, but that stance was very much in keeping with the broader American foreign policy of anti-communism. The Polish American lobby scored its greatest success after the Cold War had ended, when it helped win the American government's support for including Poland in the American-led transatlantic military alliance, the North American Treaty Organization (NATO). With the end of the Cold War, however, while Poland's future mattered greatly to ethnic Poles, issues of European security had become much less important in the eyes of the American public. Polish NATO membership is therefore an instance of an interest group getting its way because the issue in question combined high intensity for a relatively small number of people with low salience for the rest of the country.[23]

Unlike the Germans, the Irish, and the Poles, Cuban immigrants to the United States organized themselves soon after they arrived, in the early 1960s. An important reason for this difference is that they were not economic migrants but rather political refugees, fleeing Fidel Castro's communist dictatorship. They pressed for a policy of robust opposition to the Castro regime, and the American government carried out such a policy throughout the Cold War. It did so, however, principally for reasons of global anti-communism: it did not need the urgings of Cuban Americans to find that regime both repugnant and threatening, particularly when it aligned itself with the Soviet Union. Indeed, the most vigorous initiative against the communist government of the Caribbean island, the failed invasion by American-sponsored anti-Castro Cuban exiles at the Bay of Pigs, took place in 1961, even before the Cuban American lobby had fully formed.

In one notable instance, ethnic lobbies conspicuously failed to bend American foreign policy to their wishes. Two of them sought to make the nation's policy less friendly to Turkey. Armenian Americans were motivated by the mass slaughter of Armenians in which the Turkish-dominated Ottoman Empire had engaged during World War I, an event that the successor to that empire, the Turkish republic, refused even to acknowledge. Greek Americans remembered the eviction of ethnic Greeks from Asia Minor after World War I, when the Turkish republic was established, and objected to Turkey's invasion of Cyprus, its mistreatment of Cypriot Greeks, and its forcible partition of that Mediterranean island in 1974.

The United States had no ties of sentiment with Turkey, which had fought on the opposing side in the First World War and remained neutral in the Second. During the Cold War, however, the American government considered Turkey a valuable ally against the Soviet Union and included it in NATO. Washington's geopolitical concerns gave Turkey protection against the efforts of two American ethnic groups to modify American policy toward it.

The ethnic lobby that has aroused the most controversy is the one supporting Israel, the nation-state of the Jewish people. According to hostile accounts of that lobby, the small segment of the national population that is Jewish has contrived to wrench the country's foreign policy out of its proper course and enlist it in support of a tiny state in the Middle East. Such accounts sometimes go beyond normal political discourse and enter the realm of conspiracy theories.[24] In fact, the record of the pro-Israel lobby conforms to the general pattern of ethnic politics: it has enjoyed success when, and because, its preferred policies have followed the broader, publicly sanctioned directions of American foreign policy as a whole.

Jews have been present in America since colonial times. Many emigrated from Germany in the middle of the nineteenth century and many more came from Eastern Europe in the last decades of that century and the beginning of the next one, but Jewish Americans have never made up more than 4 percent of the national population. In the latter decades of the nineteenth century, they persuaded the American government to protest (although not to take any concrete steps to stop) the murderous assaults against Jews in tsarist Russia.[25] In the wake of the destruction of European Jewry in World War II, an event known as the Holocaust, the state of Israel was established in the ancient Jewish homeland on the eastern shore of the Mediterranean, then a province of the British Empire known as Palestine. Before the war, American Jews had largely responded to Zionism, the movement to establish such a state, with indifference or even hostility, but afterward many supported it enthusiastically.

The United States became the second country to accord official recognition to Israel upon its establishment in 1948 (the Soviet Union was the first); but in the new state's early years, when it had the greatest need of outside support, America provided very little. In Israel's War of Independence against the five Arab armies that invaded it in 1948, the American government did not supply it with weapons. (The Israeli army did obtain some American arms through non-governmental channels.) In the Anglo–French–Israeli 1956 war with Egypt, Washington forced Israel to withdraw from positions it had gained in the fighting. In its sweeping victory over three Arab countries in June 1967, Israel relied on French, not American, arms.

Not only did Israel not receive American help when it was most needed, as the events after the 1956 War demonstrate, American Middle Eastern policy did not always favor Israel, the efforts of the pro-Israel lobby notwithstanding. In the 1980s, the lobby and the Israeli government strongly opposed the sale of a sophisticated Airborne Warning and Control System (AWACS) to the Kingdom of Saudi Arabia, fearing that it would be employed in ways that would undermine Israel's security. The sale went ahead anyway. In 2014, the lobby, the Israeli government, and a majority of the American public opposed the Obama administration's nuclear deal with the Islamic Republic of Iran known as the Joint Comprehensive Program of Action (JCPOA). That deal also went forward.

American foreign policy worked to Israel's advantage when and because the two country's domestic political values, and more importantly their strategic outlooks, were aligned. More often than not they were. During the Cold War, Israel acted as a bulwark against pro-Soviet countries and movements in the Middle East; and in that region, Israel stood out as the lone democracy. Both what it was and what it did, and not the supposed machinations of the groups lobbying on its behalf, inclined Americans of all backgrounds to be favorably disposed to the Jewish state.

The pro-Israel lobby did differ from other ethnic pressure groups in one particular way. The others consisted mainly of people with ethnic ties to the country whose interests they were attempting to promote, and like them one of the principal pro-Israel organizations, the American–Israel Public Affairs Committee (AIPAC), was composed mainly of Jews. By far the largest pro-Israel group in the United States, however, Christians United for Israel (CUFI), had a largely non-Jewish, Christian membership. CUFI supported the Jewish state for Christian, biblical reasons. A reported three million people belonged to AIPAC. The comparable number for CUFI was ten million.

POLITICAL PARTIES

The Constitution of 1788 makes no mention of political parties, and America's first president, George Washington, took a dim view of them. Nonetheless, political parties have played a central role in the public life of the United States almost from its founding. Parties have served as the vehicles for aggregating the diverse interests of the American people so that they can be translated into law and policy. Parties contest the elections by which the American people choose their leaders. Parties organize the various legislative bodies of the nation's federal system so that they can perform the task with which they are charged—that is, enacting legislation. All democratic political systems have political parties for these purposes, and it seems doubtful that a modern democracy could function without them.

Compared with other democracies, the United States has had unusually large and unusually long-lived political parties. It has also almost always had two major parties. One of them, now called the Democratic Party but at its origins in the early nineteenth century known as the Republicans and called by historians the Democratic-Republicans, has maintained a continuous existence from its founding to the present. The other major party has gone through three incarnations: first as the Federalists, then as the Whigs, and finally, from the mid-nineteenth century to the twenty-first, as the Republicans.[26] The domestic interests the two have represented have remained roughly constant over the centuries: the Democrats have been the party of outsiders, while their opponents consisted of whatever counted as the American establishment of the day.[27] The Democrats have generally spoken for the less well-to-do, the Republicans and their ancestors for the more affluent. As the Industrial Revolution took hold in the United States, the Democrats increasingly embraced the cause of labor, the Republicans that of capital.[28]

On matters of foreign and military policy, clear differences have usually divided the two parties, but over time the two have sometimes traded places in their general orientations. From the beginning of the nineteenth century to the Civil War, the Democratic-Republicans had greater enthusiasm for territorial expansion, including the use of force to achieve it, than did their partisan adversaries. In the wake of the Civil War, the Republicans generally favored a more assertive foreign policy. In the twentieth century, however, Democratic presidents led the country into the two world wars and the Cold War, sometimes over Republican objections. In the 1960s, the Republicans became more and the Democrats less amenable to a vigorous American role in the world.[29]

Although the political parties have represented the views of the American public, they have not acted simply as the means of transmission for those views; they have shaped Americans' views on foreign policy as well. Each party has been a broad coalition, some of whose members have joined it on the basis of domestic issues and have had weakly held opinions, or none at all, on issues of foreign policy.[30] When that has been the case, they have often adopted the prevailing views of the party that they have chosen to join on the basis of other issues.

One study of public opinion on war and peace in the middle third of the twentieth century divided Americans into three categories, according to the source of their attitudes toward the conflicts in Korea and Vietnam:[31] partisans, who took their cues from party leaders; followers, influenced by national opinion leaders, especially the president; and believers, who based their views on what they knew about the issues in question. Since the president is also the leader of his party, people in two of the three categories followed the lead of their political parties.[32]

Not only partisan affiliation but also partisan conflict has affected the conduct of American foreign policy. "Politics stops at the water's edge" is a familiar refrain in the discourse of public affairs in the United States, but it happens not to describe the country's foreign policy for most of its history.[33] Partisan divisions, and their effects on the nation's relations with the rest of the world, count as one of the ways in which America has conducted an exceptionally democratic foreign policy.

The political cleavage that gave rise to the first two opposing political parties had its roots in an event outside North America—the French Revolution. The Democratic-Republicans came together in no small part on the basis of their enthusiasm for that epochal historical event. They did so under the leadership of Thomas Jefferson, a Francophile who became the nation's third president. The Federalists, by contrast, reacted to the French Revolution, and especially to the terror and the imperial expansion that followed the overthrow of the king, with emotions ranging from distaste to horror. In the Anglo–French conflict at the heart of the wars that followed the Revolution, the Federalists favored the British. The Democratic-Republicans became, in varying degrees, disappointed by the course the Revolution took but remained steadfastly opposed to Great Britain.[34] Their opposition, heightened by what the Democratic-Republicans (and other Americans) regarded as British violations of America's maritime neutral rights, led ultimately to war against Great Britain in 1812.

The War of 1812 was, on the American side, a partisan affair. The Democratic-Republicans voted for it in Congress,[35] and a president of their party, James Madison—Thomas Jefferson's political heir—presided over it. The Federalists, on the other hand, adamantly opposed waging war against the British.[36]

The war went badly for the United States and severely divided the country, creating considerable ill will toward the government on the part of the war's opponents.[37] The American armed forces performed, on the whole, badly. The British invaded the country and occupied and set fire to its capital, Washington, DC. When the war finally ended, with the Treaty of Ghent of December 1814, the United States gained nothing. The Treaty restored the prewar status quo in virtually every important way.[38]

Such an outcome should have redounded to the political advantage of the Federalists, who had, after all, objected to what seems, in retrospect, to have been a fiasco. In fact, the opposite occurred. The American public came to see the war as a success—a "second war of independence"[39]— and the Democratic-Republicans who were responsible for it became the dominant force in American politics. The Federalists faded politically and then disappeared entirely.[40]

The Democrats (as the Democratic-Republicans had become in 1828) also favored, and initiated, the war against Mexico in 1846. That war was a personal project of the Democratic president James K. Polk. If the Democrats had not held the presidency, and perhaps even if a different Democrat had been president, the war would not have taken place. Although the opposition Whigs, who had succeeded the Federalists, voted against the Mexican War—a young Whig congressman, Abraham Lincoln, called it "a war of conquest fought to catch votes"[41]—they took to heart the fate of the Federalists and did not mount a full-scale campaign to thwart Polk's policy.[42] While criticizing the president and blocking some of his war measures, they consistently voted for funds to support the troops in the field.[43] This strategy of hedging brought political rewards as the war's popularity declined. The Whigs did well in the midterm congressional elections of 1846[44] and won the presidency in 1848 with Zachary Taylor, a Mexican War general, as their nominee.[§]

The Civil War divided the country by region, but within the Union partisan differences impinged on the federal government's policies. The Northern Democrats, who had remained loyal to the Union while their Southern counterparts seceded, had major disagreements with the way that Abraham Lincoln, now a Republican and the president of what remained of the United States, was conducting the conflict. Many Democrats did not favor the emancipation of the slaves in the rebellious Southern states that the president proclaimed on the first day of 1863.[45] The next year, many of them wanted a compromise peace with the Confederacy; and had the Democratic candidate, the former Union army general George McClellan, won the presidential election of that year—something that Lincoln feared would happen until Union military victories in the South during the summer brightened his electoral prospects—the war might have ended in that way.[46]

A president from Lincoln's party, William McKinley, presided over the Spanish–American War of 1898, and the enthusiasm for that war among officeholders came largely from Republican ranks. The Democrats had reservations about it but lacked the political strength to prevent either the invasion of Cuba or the subsequent, and more controversial, annexation of the Philippines.

World War I did not sharply polarize the country on partisan lines, but the proposal that the United States join the League of Nations, the organization that President Woodrow Wilson had taken the lead in designing at the postwar peace conference in Paris, did divide Democrats from Republicans. Massachusetts Senator Henry Cabot Lodge, the leader of the Republicans in the Senate and the League's chief American opponent, had several reasons for his opposition. He was skeptical that the League would work to keep the peace as Wilson believed it would. He

---

[§] The Mexican War followed a political trajectory that would be repeated in the Korean, Vietnam, and Iraq Wars of the twentieth and twenty-first centuries. All were popular at the beginning, all lost popularity as they wore on, and the opposition party—the Republicans for Korea and Vietnam, the Democrats for Iraq—were able to take political advantage of the fall in public support. See pp. 122–123.

harbored a deep personal animosity toward the president. He also had a partisan motive: he saw an advantage for his party in preventing Wilson from recording what, if the United States had joined the League, the president would have regarded as his greatest achievement.[47] The majority of Republicans voted against the version of the League of Nations that Wilson championed, and the effort to include the United States in it failed—the victim, among other things, of partisan domestic politics.

Like World War I, World War II—once the United States formally entered it—did not divide Americans along partisan lines. President Franklin Roosevelt had taken steps in advance to mute partisan friction by bringing prominent Republicans into his administration in positions of major responsibility: Henry Stimson, who had served as secretary of state under Theodore Roosevelt, Franklin's cousin and Republican predecessor, became secretary of war. Frank Knox, the Republican vice-presidential candidate in 1936, was appointed secretary of the navy.[48] Franklin Roosevelt thereby produced an innovation in his country's foreign policy: bipartisanship.

Its spirit and practice continued through the first two decades of the Cold War but came close to being derailed in 1952. In that year, two major candidates competed for the Republican presidential nomination. Dwight D. Eisenhower, who had served in World War II as the Supreme Allied Commander in Europe and later as the military leader of NATO, endorsed the policy of forceful global opposition to the Soviet Union and communism worldwide, and an American security guarantee to the countries of Western Europe for that purpose, that the Truman administration had inaugurated. His opponent, Robert Taft, a prominent member of the Senate from Ohio (and son of former president William Howard Taft) preferred a more restrained foreign policy, with more modest overseas military and political commitments than the United States had made since the end of World War II. Eisenhower secured the nomination and went on to win the election. His administration continued the foreign policies of its Democratic predecessor, as a Taft presidency might well not have done.

During the Cold War, partisan differences had a significant impact on presidential contests on two occasions. Both John F. Kennedy in 1960 and Ronald Reagan in 1980 supported the general Cold War policy of deterring and containing the Soviet Union, but both accused the incumbent administration of the other party of failing to wage the contest with communism with sufficient energy and determination.[49] The United States, each all but said, was losing the Cold War. Kennedy and Reagan were both elected, and both proceeded to make good their common promise to prosecute the conflict with communism more vigorously in various ways, notably in both cases by increasing defense spending.

Between 1960 and 1980 came the Vietnam War, which affected the major parties' approaches to America's relations with the rest of the world in two ways. First, it brought the post-1945 consensus on foreign policy to an end. The divisions that began in Vietnam continued for the next four decades, with the gap between the parties becoming widest during the Iraq War that began in 2003.[50] Second, as a result of Vietnam in their foreign-policy orientations the two parties traded places. The Democrats became less disposed to conduct an assertive foreign policy: they became, to use a term that gained currency in that era, more dovish. The Republicans traveled in the opposite direction, becoming more hawkish.

The Vietnam experience demonstrated, among other things, that war is a foreign-policy event that engages the entire country, the occasion on which public opinion as a whole has a major bearing on the direction of the country's policy. In that war, public sentiment ultimately worked to terminate active American military engagement in Southeast Asia. It ended the Vietnam War for the United States. On other occasions it has had the contrary effect. Public opinion has sometimes pushed America toward, or even into, armed conflict.

PUBLIC OPINION AND WAR: TAILWINDS

A disinclination to go to war is built into American society. The founders of the United States believed that the political system they established would conduct itself peacefully in its relations with other countries. Many of the immigrants who arrived from Europe and elsewhere over the course of the nation's history were seeking to escape the bellicose governments of their original countries and the wars these governments waged. In the twentieth century, the thesis that democracies do not go to war, at least not with one another, gained currency in the United States, including among its leaders.[51] For all that, however, an aversion to war has not always dominated American public life or American foreign policy.

In fact, a particular pattern propelling the nation in the opposite direction has recurred throughout American history. The pattern begins with a dramatic event—usually abroad but occasionally within the United States itself—that seizes the attention of the American public and suddenly makes the world seem more dangerous. This leads to a broadly shared demand for a new and more robust policy to meet the new (or newly recognized) danger, a demand that the people actually responsible for conducting foreign policy have often shared. Sometimes the new policy has turned out to be war.[**]

War has followed direct attacks on the United States—against the federal military facility at Fort Sumter, South Carolina, on April 12, 1861, for example, and in New York City and Washington, DC, on September 11, 2001—because on such occasions the country was, in effect, already at war; others had forced war upon the United States. Another long-remembered such instance, and one with momentous geopolitical consequences, came on December 7, 1941, when Japan attacked the naval base at Pearl Harbor, Hawaii. The congressional declaration of war the next day followed more or less automatically.[52]

Galvanizing events other than direct attacks have not always led directly to war, but instead have shifted national perceptions and national

---

[**] One consequence of this recurrent pattern is that the sharpest changes of direction in American foreign policy have usually come about not through changes of administration—when control of the executive branch passes from one party to the other—but rather when a dramatic event compels a sitting administration to alter its course. Michael Mandelbaum, *The Four Ages of American Foreign Policy: Weak Power, Great Power, Superpower, Hyperpower*, New York: Oxford University Press, 2022, p. 343. For example, the administration of George W. Bush entered office promising a humbler, more modest foreign policy than its predecessor had conducted, but then waged war and undertook elaborate efforts at state-building in two distant countries, Afghanistan and Iraq, as the result of the terrorist attacks on New York City and Washington, DC, of September 11, 2001.

attitudes in ways that have made war more likely. A concept known as the Overton Window[53] refers to the range of policies on a particular issue that is acceptable to the public at any given time.[54] Politicians who advocate policies that fall outside this range risk being dismissed as unserious or even voted out of office because their views are too extreme. Dramatic events in American history have had the effect of shifting the Overton Window to make assertive foreign policies, including the use of force, that were previously considered unacceptable suddenly plausible. On September 10, 2001, no American official had suggested fighting a war in Afghanistan. On September 12, virtually all of them supported doing so after terrorists based in that country launched attacks on two American cities that killed almost 3,000 people.

Americans have been historically susceptible to the mind-changing force of dramatic events because human beings in general are susceptible to them. Pictures speak louder than words; events move people in ways that ideas do not.[55] In addition, some of the particular features of the United States have enhanced its citizens' susceptibility to abrupt and sweeping changes in mood about the rest of the world. For most of its history, geography made the country unusually secure. Americans paid little attention to events beyond their borders because they had no compelling personal reasons to do so. Since imminent dangers were almost always nonexistent, when one did appear, or seemed to appear, it came as a nasty shock. Moreover, many Americans have been culturally and temperamentally inclined to lash out at what has suddenly loomed as a threat.[56] Content under ordinary circumstances to be left alone, they have responded fiercely to perceived intrusions. A slogan from the Revolutionary War era, "Don't tread on me," which appeared on a flag with a picture of a coiled rattlesnake ready to strike, expressed this attitude. Once trod upon, Americans through the centuries have reacted forcefully.

The first American war, the colonial rebellion against the British Empire, only partly fits that template. It had its origins in a series of political measures—taxes imposed from London that the colonials considered unjust—that provoked indignation rather than alarm and made the world seem unjust rather than positively dangerous. Two violent episodes did, however, help to push the Americans to armed conflict: the Boston Massacre of March 5, 1770, in which British troops opened fire on a hostile mob and killed several of its members;[57] and the skirmishes between British regular forces and colonial militiamen in the Massachusetts towns of Lexington and Concord on April 19, 1775, which turned out to be the first battles of the Revolutionary War.

The War of 1812 lacked a single galvanizing event. British seizures of American ships caused the conflict,[58] but that practice, which did arouse American anger, stretched over almost two decades and was punctuated by diplomatic efforts to resolve the dispute and Thomas Jefferson's embargo before the ongoing British policy finally triggered an American declaration of war.

The Mexican War of 1846–1848 did begin with a dramatic, attention-seizing event, although it was at least partly contrived by an American president bent on territorial expansion and willing to wage war for that purpose.[59] The United States and Mexico disagreed about the location of the border between Mexico and Texas. President Polk sent American troops into the disputed territory, Mexican soldiers fired on them, and the Polk administration, asserting that American forces had been attacked on American soil, treated this as a cause of war. The American public agreed, regarding the episode as an outrage and provocation. Support for a punitive military expedition against Mexico soared,[60] and the American army received a flood of volunteers.

The Civil War could hardly have come as a complete surprise to the citizens of the Northern states that remained loyal to the Union, since slavery had divided the country with increasing bitterness since its founding and the Southern states had seceded from the Union following the election of Abraham Lincoln as president in 1860. Still, the Confederate attack on Fort Sumter made a sharp impression on the Northern states, which gave Lincoln a basis for mobilizing them for war.[61]

In the next major American armed conflict, against Spain in 1898, another dramatic event played an important role. Americans were appalled by Spain's mistreatment of the Cubans they ruled and who had risen against them, and more and more Yankees came to believe that the United States should intervene to rescue the Cubans.[62] Then, on February 15, 1898, the battleship *Maine*, which Washington had dispatched to the Havana harbor as a show of concern and support for the Cubans, exploded and sank. Although subsequently diagnosed as an accident, the explosion was widely believed at the time to be the work of the Spanish, and thus an attack by Spain on the United States. This perception helped to push an initially reluctant President William McKinley to ask for a declaration of war against Spain.[63]

Another ship-sinking, seventeen years after the *Maine* exploded, set in motion a chain of events at the end of which the United States entered World War I. When a German submarine sank the British passenger liner *Lusitania* on May 7, 1915, killing 1,195 of the people on board, Americans were shocked and angered, not least because 123 of their countrymen were among the dead. The episode turned the American public against Germany. Woodrow Wilson, who wanted his country to stay out of the European war, demanded that the Germans halt their submarine warfare and all but guaranteed that the United States would enter the war against Germany if they did not.[64] The Germans did stop submarine attacks on surface ships for a time, but in early 1917 renewed the practice and the United States responded by declaring war.[65]

While it was the Japanese attack on Pearl Harbor that propelled the United States into the next world war, a dramatic event that took place eighteen months before December 7, 1941, had a powerful impact on the American approach to the fighting underway in Europe. The fall of France to a German assault that routed the French army in June 1940 came as a grim surprise: the French had, after all, held out against the German army in the previous European conflict for four long years. The German conquest made the world seem a suddenly more dangerous place, not least to President Roosevelt, who would almost certainly not have sought, or won, a third presidential term in 1940 had the European war not proceeded as it did in that year.[66]

France's defeat shifted the Overton Window for America's Europe policy. It made the American public decidedly more willing than before to send military assistance to the countries resisting Nazi Germany, which the Roosevelt administration proceeded to do, although Americans were not (yet) willing to enter the war themselves.[67]

Five years after World War II ended, the United States went to war again, this time on the Korean peninsula. Once again, a galvanizing event—a surprise attack on South Korea by the army of communist North Korea on June 25, 1950—transformed the foreign policy of the United States. The dispatch of American troops to help the South resist the North was in one sense surprising. Korea was distant, unfamiliar to almost all Americans, and economically unimportant; and before June 1950 the American government had displayed little interest in its fate. President Truman decided to intervene because he regarded the North Korean attack on the South as a repetition of the tactics Nazi Germany had employed in Europe in the 1930s, which had led to World War II. The communists, he believed, like the Nazis before them, were intent on moving against the democracies step by step and had to be stopped, as the Nazis had not been, to prevent a wider, more costly conflict.[68]

The attack made the public far more willing to support an American war in East Asia than it would otherwise have been. To be sure, by June 1950 the global rivalry with the Soviet Union and its communist allies and clients was well underway. For the United States, however, at that point the Cold War was primarily a European political conflict. The Korean War made it a military undertaking, and an Asian one as well.

In 1957, another dramatic international event made the world abruptly appear to Americans a more perilous place. The Soviet launch of the first earth-orbiting satellite, called Sputnik, seemed to give the communist side in the Cold War a distinct advantage in a militarily significant area—outer space. Sputnik did not lead to war, but it did sufficiently alarm the American people to persuade them to increase national spending on defense.[69]

While the Vietnam War resembled the Korean conflict in important ways, it did not begin with a single, attention-riveting event. Instead, the United States increased its troop presence in that country gradually, over several years.[70] Four years after the conclusion of that war with the conquest of the non-communist South by the communist North in 1975—the last American soldier having left the country several years before—came the next policy-altering dramatic event in the history of American foreign policy. The Soviet Union's invasion and occupation of Afghanistan in December 1979 abruptly changed American policy in that part of the world in a way reminiscent of the national response to the fall of France. Americans did not develop an appetite for engaging in combat themselves in Afghanistan, but did send military supplies to the Afghans resisting the Soviet occupation.[71]

As had happened in Korea four decades earlier, in August 1990 an unexpected cross-border attack, this one by Iraq against its small, oil-rich neighbor Kuwait, drew the United States into a war. As with Korea, few Americans had any familiarity with Kuwait before the Iraqi invasion. Nor did the United States have Cold War reasons for proceeding as it did to forge a broad international coalition and send half a million troops to the Persian Gulf region to evict Iraq from Kuwait: the Cold War was all but over. Precisely because the conflict with global communism was ending, the administration of George H. W. Bush saw the invasion as an opportunity to establish post–Cold War international norms reflecting American values, including a norm against committing aggression of the kind that Iraq had carried out. The administration also had a geopolitical reason for the diplomatic and military initiatives it took: had the Iraqi dictator Saddam Hussein been allowed to keep Kuwait, he would then have menaced Saudi Arabia, the largest source of the oil on which the global economy depended.[72]

The attacks on New York City and Washington, DC, that occurred a decade after the first Gulf War, on September 11, 2001, have the distinction of giving rise to two American wars. One took place in Afghanistan. It was waged to expel the terrorist organization, al Qaeda, that had launched the attacks from its safe haven in that country. A year and a half later, in March 2003, American armed forces attacked and occupied Iraq, where Saddam continued to hold power. Some Americans believed that he had had a hand in the September 11 assaults,[73] but no evidence of direct Iraqi involvement in them ever came to light.

The administration of George W. Bush, the son of the man who had presided over the first Gulf War, took the country to war again in that region because, having failed to anticipate the terrorist attacks despite being well aware of al Qaeda and its designs, American officials asked themselves what other threats they might be underestimating and thereby placing the country in jeopardy. They concluded that Saddam and his regime belonged in that category and decided to remove him in order to forestall the serious damage to the international order and American interests he seemed willing and able to do.[74]

The second Bush administration was able to undertake the second conflict because the attacks of September 11 had shifted the Overton Window for war. Before that date, although Saddam was as unpopular with Americans as any figure in the world, sending an American expeditionary force to oust him was not politically feasible. Afterward, it was. To employ a different metaphor, the terrorist attacks supplied the American president with enough political capital to support two significant wars.[75]

Widely distributed over time and space though they were, the galvanizing events that created a demand for more assertive foreign policies over the course of American history all had two common features. First, Americans saw them as acts of aggression—against their interests if not directly against them personally. For that reason, most Americans considered the wars into which these events led them to be defensive in intent, and therefore morally and politically justified. Second, when wars have followed such galvanizing episodes, the American public has initially supported the war effort, a syndrome known to students of American public opinion as the "rally 'round the flag" effect. That initially favorable sentiment, however, did not always persist as the wars continued. Indeed, American public opinion has at least as often restrained as it has promoted war.

PUBLIC OPINION AND WAR: HEADWINDS

The aversion to war, which is at least as deeply rooted in the American character as the periodic enthusiasm for waging it, has expressed itself over the course of the nation's history in three different ways. First, public resistance to armed conflict has prevented the United States from engaging in it, or at least delayed entry into wars the country did ultimately fight. Public disinclination for war of this kind has sometimes come from negative experiences in conflicts in recent memory. Second, during wartime, presidents, who are invariably acutely aware of the potential for public opinion to turn against their war policies, and thus themselves, have taken initiatives that had as their purpose preempting public discontent and bolstering support for continuing to wage the conflict that was underway. Third, the fears of the commander-in-chief that prompted these initiatives have sometimes come to pass: the American public has turned against wars even as its armed forces were waging them. This change of national mind has usually stemmed from the cost to the United States of the ongoing conflict—a cost typically measured in casualties—that the public has come to consider too high. Ultimately, the loss of public confidence has ended American wars.

For a hundred years after the end of the War of 1812, the United States remained aloof from the wars of the European great powers, and when World War I began in 1914, the American public all but unanimously wanted to follow that well-established pattern and keep out of it.[76] Tradition, and the natural desire to steer clear of trouble, accounted for the public reluctance to become directly involved in the conflict. Even after the sinking of *Lusitania*, the American people maintained what President Woodrow Wilson called a "double wish": to defend the country's neutral rights, which they believed Germany to be infringing, while avoiding the fighting themselves.[77] As for Wilson himself, for the first part of the war he made his primary goal not the victory of one side or the other but rather a state of affairs at its end that would permit him to lead an effort to abolish war entirely—a task he took up at the Paris Peace Conference. Wilson did not lead the effort to take the United States into the war. It was public opinion, responding to German submarine warfare, that made America an active belligerent.

Franklin D. Roosevelt had a different attitude toward World War II than Wilson had had toward World War I. Roosevelt very strongly favored the British cause and regarded the prospect of a German victory with alarm. He did what he could to support Great Britain (and later the Soviet Union) before Pearl Harbor, but public opinion limited his freedom of maneuver.[78] The resistance he encountered stemmed from the American public's retrospective disenchantment with their country's participation in the First World War. Americans came to regard that war as a mistake.[79] It had not made Europe an oasis of peace, as Americans had hoped. The Europeans had borrowed a great deal of money from the United States during the war, and many Americans resented what seemed to be the debtors' resistance to repaying what they owed.[80] In addition, some Americans came to believe that the political settlement devised at the Paris Peace Conference had treated Germany unfairly. For these reasons, any measure that seemed to move the United States closer to full-scale engagement in the European conflict aroused opposition.[81]

The British government and the British public shared some of Americans' reservations about World War I and had, as well, a horror of becoming involved in another such war given how much the last one had cost them in lives and money. Great Britain therefore attempted to conciliate Nazi Germany through a policy that came to be known as appeasement. Separated from Europe by 3,000 miles of ocean, the United States could and did respond to Germany's dismantling of the post–World War I settlement on the Continent with detachment, as the American public wished. Britain, with only the English Channel—twenty-one miles wide at its narrowest point—between itself and Europe, did not have that luxury.

Unlike the First World War, the Second came to be seen as a success. The Korean War, although it ended in a stalemate, did not count as a failure. The American public did come to see the Vietnam War as a failure, however, with majorities saying, even before it ended, that waging it had been a mistake. That perception gave rise to what came to be known as the "Vietnam Syndrome"—an extreme reluctance on the part of the public to commit American troops to battle because of what had happened in Southeast Asia.[82]

American soldiers did not fight anywhere in large numbers for the two decades after the final withdrawal of American ground troops from Southeast Asia in 1972, and the Vietnam Syndrome was in evidence in the 1980s when the Reagan administration supported an insurgency against the communist-sympathizing dictatorship in the Central American country of Nicaragua. The military operations of the Contras, as the insurgents were called, took place on a small scale. The United States had intervened in the region many times and had long maintained a proprietary interest there on the basis of the Monroe Doctrine of 1823. The administration showed no inclination to send American troops to fight alongside the Contras. Despite all this, substantial opposition even to supplying the insurgents with weapons and money made itself felt in the country and in Congress. The opposition wanted no part of any policy that had even a remote chance of leading to a Vietnam-like entanglement.[83] When, in 1991, the United States did send troops to fight abroad and achieved its goal of evicting the Iraqi army from Kuwait in 1991, President George H. W. Bush exclaimed, "By God, we've kicked the Vietnam Syndrome once and for all!"[84]

The second war in the Persian Gulf, twelve years later, which became as unpopular as the Vietnam War had been, reinstated the aversion to putting American troops in harm's way that the Vietnam experience had created. What might be called the "Iraq Syndrome"[85] played a role in the policy adopted by the administration of President Barack Obama, who was elected in 2008 as an opponent of the Iraq War, of conciliating the Islamic Republic of Iran. Obama believed, wrongly as it turned out, that diplomacy, including financial incentives, would reduce, if not eliminate, the Iranian regime's vociferously and consistently proclaimed hostility to the United States. In 2015, his administration negotiated some limits on Iran's nuclear-weapons program, an agreement known as the Joint Comprehensive Plan of Action (JCPOA). Modest in scope, and with the limits that it imposed due, by the terms to which the American government agreed, to expire after a few years, the JCPOA met with the disapproval of a plurality of Americans. Obama defended it by invoking the specter of Iraq in declaring that the alternative to it was war.[86]

During wartime, all presidents have paid close attention to public opinion. A wartime American commander-in-chief has a number of responsibilities, one of which—not the least important of them and sometimes the most difficult—is to keep the American public committed to whatever war the nation is fighting. To that end, presidents have sometimes adopted policies designed to fortify public support for the ongoing conflict and thus, ultimately, to enhance the president's capacity to wage it. Such presidential initiatives occurred during the Mexican War, the Civil War, and World War II.[87]

In the war with Mexico, President James K. Polk sent a representative, Nicholas Trist, to negotiate a peace settlement with the Mexican government. Polk then decided to insist on harsher terms, with more territory ceded to the United States, than Trist had been authorized to offer. Acting on his own, Trist proposed the original conditions to the Mexican authorities,[88] and they accepted. His insubordination angered Polk, but because the war had lost popularity as it proceeded, making domestic support for continuing it increasingly shaky,[89] the president decided to accept the Treaty of Guadalupe Hidalgo that Trist's negotiations had produced.[90] The act of insubordination established the southern border of the United States.

Perhaps the most significant political initiative in the course of the Civil War was President Abraham Lincoln's issuance, on the first day of 1863, of the Emancipation Proclamation, which freed all the slaves in the Confederacy. Lincoln had several motives for his decree.[91] They included enhancing support for the increasingly costly war not only in the Northern states but also among the British public, whose sentiments helped to determine British policy toward the war.[92] That policy, in turn, was crucial for both sides. The Emancipation Proclamation heartened, and expanded enthusiasm for the war among, the people in the North who ardently sought the end of slavery—the abolitionists. It also succeeded in tilting opinion in Great Britain, where slavery was unpopular and throughout whose empire it had been abolished in 1833, in a direction favorable to the Union cause.[93]

Finally, in World War II, Franklin Roosevelt decided that the first major military operation of the American armed forces would take place in North Africa. His generals regarded such a campaign as an unwarranted diversion from the main business of the war in Europe, which was to attack and defeat Nazi Germany. Operation Torch went ahead anyway, with the first American landings taking place on November 8, 1942. Roosevelt authorized the North African campaign because he believed that, in order to sustain public support for the war that had begun for the United States eleven months earlier, the American people had to see their army in action in the calendar year 1942.[94] American forces were not yet numerous enough, or sufficiently well-trained or experienced, to conduct a direct assault on northern Europe, which did not occur until more than a year and a half later, in June 1944. So the president chose North Africa. He based his decision on a political calculation, one that he, as a practicing politician, had better credentials for making than his military advisors.

Hard as they may have tried, American presidents have not always eliminated domestic opposition to the wars over which they have presided. Indeed, and to be accurate, no president has ever managed to accomplish this. All of the nation's wars, without exception, have aroused opposition of one kind or another. Dissent is as American as apple pie.

In the first war, against the British Empire, protest took the form of emigration. Residents of the thirteen colonies who did not support the rebellion against Great Britain—an estimated 80,000 of them—moved (or fled) to Canada or other British colonies (or to Great Britain itself), where they could continue to live as loyal British subjects.[95]

The War of 1812 aroused widespread and active opposition, above all in New England. The second war against Great Britain has a good claim to being the most unpopular one the United States ever fought.[96] Some of the opposition verged on subversion of the war effort, and in December 1814 and January 1815 representatives of the New England states convened at Hartford, Connecticut, to discuss their grievances against the national government. The Hartford Convention seemed at the time, at least to some, to be a prelude to secession.[97] When the war ended, the opposition dissipated, and the Federalist Party, which expressed that opposition, disappeared.[98]

Dissent in the Mexican War took three forms: moral objections, most common in New England, to the assault on Mexico, whose best-known exponent historically, Henry David Thoreau of Massachusetts, wrote his subsequently famous essay "On Civil Disobedience" to disseminate his views; rising public dissatisfaction with the conduct of the war because of its length and costs, discontent whose precise scope could not and cannot be assessed with precision because scientific polling did not exist in the nineteenth century but whose existence is evident in the results of the elections of 1846 and 1848, in both of which President Polk's Democrats fared poorly; and finally, the policies of the Whig Party, which took political advantage of the moral objections and public discontent in those elections.[99]

During the Civil War, a faction of the Democratic Party that had remained loyal to the Union known as the Copperheads favored a peace settlement with the Confederacy.[100] Congress included several members of this faction, most notably Clement Vallandigham of Ohio. President Lincoln insisted on prosecuting the war until victory was achieved; but had the Union armies not scored major victories in the South in 1864, the Democrats might have won the presidential election of that year and carried out the Copperheads' preferred course.

In 1898, the invasion of Cuba provoked little opposition in the United States. Most Americans regarded it as a mission to rescue the Cuban people, and the fighting on the island went well from the American point of view. The consequence of that war on the other side of the world, however—the annexation of the Philippines that made that Pacific Ocean archipelago an American imperial possession—was a different matter. Congress was evenly divided on annexation: a resolution declaring the Philippines independent ended in a tie, with the vote of the vice president breaking the deadlock to ensure the resolution's rejection. The wealthy industrialist Andrew Carnegie subsidized the formation of an Anti-Imperialist League that opposed the creation of an American empire chiefly on the grounds that it violated basic American political values. Prominent citizens such as the novelist Mark Twain and the philosopher William James lent their names to the League.[101]

World War I came closest to being a dissent-free American war, in part because there was comparatively little war to protest: American troops were engaged in combat in France for only eight months. That did not, however, prevent the federal government from enacting legislation designed to discourage and even suppress dissent through the Espionage Act of 1917 and the Sedition Act of 1918, and to incarcerate several dissidents, including the perennial Socialist Party candidate for president, Eugene V. Debs.

Vigorous opposition to American participation in World War II did make itself known, but almost entirely before the United States formally entered the conflict. The America First Committee, whose most prominent member was the aviator Charles A. Lindbergh—famous for having been, in 1927, the first man to fly alone across the Atlantic Ocean— became a major presence in the nation's public life between September 1940 and the American declaration of war in December 1941, after which it was disbanded.[102]

In the seven decades after the end of World War II in 1945, the United States waged three significant wars—in Korea, Vietnam, and Iraq. Only the Vietnam conflict called forth an active, visible antiwar movement, but in other respects domestic opposition to the three, and the political effects of that opposition, followed the same pattern.[103]

Each commanded broad support at the outset, but as it proceeded, support diminished. Those belonging to the political party that did not control the White House, and thus not responsible for the conduct of the war, tended to abandon support for it first. Republicans turned against wars managed by Democrats, and vice versa. Ultimately, a majority of the public came to believe waging war in Vietnam and Iraq to have been mistakes.

American opponents of American wars, especially in the nineteenth century, have sometimes believed that their country was fighting for unworthy goals. That was not the case for Korea, Vietnam, and Iraq. Few among the public repudiated the goals for which the wars were being fought. The American people continued to endorse, in principle, keeping South Korea and South Vietnam free of communist control and the creation of a decent government in post–Saddam Hussein Iraq. They turned against the policy of continuing the wars because they decided that the costs of doing so had become higher than was acceptable.[104]

The public measured the cost of the wars principally in American casualties, above all combat deaths.[††] Americans expressed their

[††] John E. Mueller, *War and Ideas: Selected Essays*, New York: Routledge, 2011, p. 172. The total number of deaths in Iraq was considerably lower than in Korea and Vietnam, but public

dissatisfaction in each case by voting against the political party, and its president, responsible for the war. In the presidential elections of 1952, 1968, and 2012, the out-party's candidates—Dwight D. Eisenhower, Richard M. Nixon, and Barack H. Obama—won the presidency with a promise to end American military involvement in Korea, Vietnam, and Iraq, respectively. Upon taking office, each proceeded to do so.

Through their votes in each case, the American public was able to change a war policy of which a majority had come to disapprove. In this way, the Korean, Vietnam, and Iraq Wars, while varying widely in their consequences for the United States and the world, have one feature in common: each illustrates the third major and continuing theme in America's history—the democratic character of its foreign policy.

tolerance for casualties was also lower for Iraq than for the two Asian wars. This was presumably because, by the time of the Iraq War, the Cold War had ended and the United States was not, as it had been in Asia, fighting an adversary that threatened the United States directly. "[A]fter two years of war [in Korea, Vietnam, and Iraq] support for war ... had slumped to around 50 percent. However, at that point around 20,000 Americans had been killed in Vietnam and Korea, but only about 1,500 in Iraq. Korea and Vietnam were seen, initially at least, to be important and necessary components in dealing with international Communism." *Ibid.*, p. 200.

The three enduring features of American foreign policy—its unusually ideological, unusually economic, and unusually democratic approach to relations with other countries—pervade the history of that foreign policy from the eighteenth century to the twenty-first. Their influence has been continually in evidence since even before the founding of the republic. What impact have these three characteristics had, not only on the United States but also beyond its borders—that is, on the whole world? The three differ in important ways, which means that assessing their impact raises different sets of questions.

The ideological aspect of the nation's foreign policy has given it a particular goal: the spread of American political ideas, so that they shape the policies, practices, and political institutions of other countries as widely and as deeply as possible. The question this raises is how far these ideas have spread, and to the extent that they have had an influence, what contribution has American foreign policy made to it.

The economic character of American foreign policy has involved the use of economic instruments to accomplish the various political goals the United States has set for itself abroad. Here the question is how well these instruments have done in achieving these goals, and how, if at all, their use has affected the world more broadly.

The third enduring feature of American foreign policy, its democratic character, has to do with the policymaking process. The question an assessment of its impact raises is whether this feature has served the nation's foreign policy well. From the early days of the United States, its inevitably democratic method of policymaking has inspired the criticism that it degrades the effectiveness of the nation's policies beyond its borders. Does the almost 250-year history of American foreign policy bear out this criticism?

***

When the United States was founded, its political ideas had very little purchase outside the settlements along the east coast of North America and the British Isles, where they had originated. The protection of individual rights formed no part of the political order almost everywhere else.[*] Thus, one-half of what constitutes modern democracy—liberty—was largely missing. So, too, was the other half: most of the world's people, and the national groups to which they belonged, were part of autocratic multinational empires, which meant that popular sovereignty was also denied to them. Moreover, just as American political ideas about the rights of individuals and the proper governance of societies were not embedded in the fabric of the political life of the planet in the last quarter of the eighteenth century, so America's preference for relations between and among sovereign states—stable, enduring peace—was neither prevalent, nor expected, nor even regarded as feasible. War and preparations for it, rather than their absence, were regarded as the permanent conditions of international relations.

By the twenty-first century, all that had changed. American political ideas had, if not entirely conquered the world, then at the very least made deep inroads into the political life of the planet.[1] The discourse of individual rights had become common. Official bodies and nongovernmental groups dedicated to their protection had proliferated. Rights flourished where democracies held sway, and by the twenty-first century much of the world had become democratic. Multinational empires had largely disappeared, affording wide opportunity for popular sovereignty. Where the people chose the government, at least as

---

[*] The exception was Great Britain, whose respect for individual rights was acknowledged by the claim, made by the colonial rebels against the British Empire, that the rebels were acting to defend what they had always had but that the British government was infringing: "the rights of Englishmen."

often as not the government honored individual liberties. As independent sovereign states grew in number, so, too—with a time lag—did the proportion of them that qualified as democratically governed.[2]

As for peace, it had become a central aspiration, at least rhetorically, among virtually all the countries of the international system, and increasingly a fact of international life as well. The number of deaths through armed conflict as a percentage of the world's population decreased.[3] Wars became rarer and, in comparison with the two world wars of the first half of the twentieth century, less deadly. One part of the world—Western Europe—which had once had the distinction of being the most violent place on earth, had become a zone of peace.

To be sure, Anglo–American political ideas did not reign supreme everywhere. Violations of individual rights outside the democracies were not rare. One large multinational empire persisted: the People's Republic of China, which forcibly subjected Muslim Uighurs and Tibetan Buddhists to Han Chinese rule. Other countries qualified as empires in miniature, with one group oppressing others. In Syria, for example, before its overthrow in 2024, the minority Alawite sect repressed the far more numerous Sunni Muslims. Even some democracies, such as Turkey and Hungary, engaged in backsliding, adopting autocratic practices.

Moreover, while the world in the twenty-first century enjoyed, by important measures, greater peace than had been the case in the eighteenth, it was not entirely peaceful. Where peace did obtain, this was sometimes due to an age-old arrangement: a stable balance of military power between and among political adversaries. In these cases, that is, peace came about through the threat of war. Overall, though, the dominant political ideas of the United States have made remarkable progress in the world since America's founding. How much of that progress has come from explicit American efforts to make the world over in its own image?

The global political transformation over two-and-one-half centuries certainly had other causes, foremost among them the two great eighteenth-century revolutions that together shaped the modern world. The French Revolution did far more to promote the ideas of individual rights and popular sovereignty than the slightly earlier American Revolution, which was a far less consequential event for the world outside North America. The Industrial Revolution—the substitution of inanimate energy for power generated by humans and animals—which began in Great Britain, spread across the planet, and continues in the present, changed every aspect of social life. The world's population became ever more urban, educated, and wealthy—all conditions that lend themselves to the adoption of the political ideas and practices that the United States has attempted to foster. The Industrial Revolution also increased the costs of war and the benefits, through economic growth, of war's absence, which has done a great deal to make the world more peaceful.[4] In addition, by making the world more democratic, the Industrial Revolution has also contributed to the spread of peace.[5]

The rise of the idea of equality has also enhanced the popularity of the political ideas America has sought to promote. In the eighteenth century, hierarchy in human affairs was considered natural, normal, even beneficial, with each person occupying his or her allotted station in life. This general idea accorded legitimacy to autocracy and empire. As inequality became less widely accepted, so too did the political practices that embodied it. The American alternative—democracy and national self-determination—correspondingly increased in legitimacy and popularity.

Human history is not, however, entirely the product of impersonal forces. Individuals and states make history as well, and because, for much of the twentieth and twenty-first centuries, the United States had more power than any other country, it had a major impact on the world's political attitudes and political architecture. Both its policies and its example—both what it did and what it was—furthered its ideological goals.

America successfully promoted its political ideas through war. Specifically, in the three great global conflicts of the twentieth century—World War I, World War II, and the Cold War—one side broadly supported, and the other opposed, liberty, democracy, and peace. The coalition supporting American ideas, which included the United States, emerged as the winner in each of the conflicts, which preserved the political systems that embodied those ideas. Success in war brings influence in times of peace, and the outcome of the three global confrontations increased the prestige and the attractiveness of the ideas, as well as the institutions and practices that followed from them, to which the United States was committed. They spread through the power of example, with America itself supplying the most potent example but not the only one. After the collapse of communism in Central and Eastern Europe, for example, the countries there chose democratic political systems because that is what the Western Europeans already had.

While the use of force successfully protected American political ideas by protecting the countries that practiced them, the power of example did far more to promote their spread to places where they were not already established. For the purpose of causing them to take root, voluntary adoption has a better record than direct or indirect coercion. When the United States was weak in comparison with other countries, in the eighteenth and nineteenth centuries, it could only hope to carry out the ideological mission it had assigned itself through the impact of its own example. In the twentieth and twenty-first centuries, it had far more power and more options for spreading its ideas; but even then, the power of example proved the most effective tactic.

✳✳✳

The United States has deployed two different types of economic instruments in pursuit of its political goals: the cross-border passage of goods and of money—that is, trade and finance. For this purpose, it has employed both sticks and carrots, in the form of sanctions and incentives. In the eighteenth and nineteenth centuries, the American use of economic instruments involved almost exclusively trade sanctions. In the twentieth and twenty-first centuries, the United States was able to add finance and incentives to its economic repertoire because its economy had grown dramatically. The country had become rich enough to export capital and to offer to foreigners attractive economic incentives involving trade as well as finance.

The use of sanctions has had mixed results at best. More often than not, the sanctions the United States has imposed in order to affect the policies of other sovereign states have not achieved their goals. They have frequently foundered on an asymmetry. Continuing the policies in question has often had a higher value for the government of the target country than causing them to stop has had for its American counterpart. The country being sanctioned has in such cases been willing to absorb the costs of the sanctions. Target countries have also often managed to mitigate the effects of sanctions by finding other sources of the imports, or customers for the exports, that the United States was seeking to deny them.[†]

The use of incentives—access to American markets and capital and direct grants and loans—has contributed to other countries' prosperity, which has generated good will toward, and underpinned geopolitical alignment with, the United States. By promoting post–World War II economic recovery in Western Europe, the Marshall Plan acted as an antidote to the political designs of local communists. In the decades after that war, Japan's economic ties with the United States reinforced the 1951 Security Treaty between the two countries.

Moreover, in the wake of the Second World War, the American use of economic instruments for political aims had an impact beyond the relations between the United States and other countries. It led to the creation of a set of international institutions, policies, and practices that decisively affected global history. Trade and capital flows grew rapidly between and among the countries that participated in the American-centered international economic order to which the international economic policies of the United States gave rise. Between the end of the war and the collapse of communism in the late 1980s and early 1990s, that order encompassed North America, Western Europe, Latin America, and much of East Asia. With the end of the Soviet Union, it became global in scope, with China and the formerly communist countries

---

[†] The colonials' trade sanctions did not end the British imperial policies to which they objected. Jefferson's embargo did not stop British infringement on what Americans regarded as their neutral rights. The Confederate embargo on cotton did not compel Great Britain to support its cause in the American Civil War. Sanctions on Japan in the years prior to World War II did not force a change in that country's policies in Asia. The embargo on Cuba did not unseat the Castro regime there. Sanctions against North Korea and Iran did not put an end to their nuclear-weapons programs.

of Europe joining it. Indeed, the superior performance of the Western economic system in comparison with the communist one helped to inspire the events that brought communism in Europe and the Soviet Union itself to an end.[6]

The United States played three important roles in this ultimately global economic system. For political as well as economic reasons, America took the lead in creating it, serving as the prime mover behind the establishment of the principal financial institution, the International Monetary Fund, and the framework for cross-border trade, the General Agreement on Tariffs and Trade. For political as well as economic reasons, America did more than any other country to keep the system functioning relatively smoothly, in particular supplying the largest market for others' exports and the main currency for international transactions, the dollar.[7] Not least important, American military power, deployed primarily for geopolitical purposes, also provided a secure backdrop for international transactions. The global American military presence imparted the confidence that is required for commerce to take place.[8] A term came into common usage to refer to the expanding volume of international trade and finance in the seventy-five years after World War II: globalization. Globalization could not and would not have taken place without the politically oriented international economic policies of the United States.

***

The democratic character of American foreign policy, with the public having unusually expansive influence over the nation's foreign relations, has manifested itself in two ways: the political system designed in the Constitution of 1788 offers multiple channels for affecting the nation's relations with other countries; and, as in all democracies, public opinion has acted as the ultimate arbiter of public policy, including foreign policy.

Almost from the beginning of the republic, each of the two has come in for criticism on the grounds that it hampers the effective promotion of America's interests beyond its borders. The existence of several centers of power in the making of foreign policy produces, it is said, a cacophony: noisy, endless, frequently inconclusive discussions and debates that confuse other countries about American intentions. The sovereignty of the public, it is also said, makes American foreign policy volatile and inconsistent, because that is the nature of public sentiment in democracies. Tocqueville regarded democratically governed countries as ill-suited to deal effectively with the world because, he said, of their propensity "to obey impulse rather than prudence," which makes it difficult for them "to persevere in a fixed design."[9]

The criticisms have some validity. The United States has at times conducted unpredictable and unsteady foreign policies that have had unwanted and unfortunate consequences. Other countries have regularly misread American intentions and failed to anticipate the force—sometimes, more accurately, the ferocity—of the American response to initiatives they have taken. Thus, the Japanese did not expect the kind of war the United States waged after Pearl Harbor.[10] The Soviet leader Josef Stalin and his communist counterpart in North Korea, Kim Il-sung, did not anticipate that, after North Korea invaded the South, the Truman administration would send a large army to the Korean peninsula to oppose the invasion.[11] Stalin's successor, Nikita Khrushchev, did not foresee the Kennedy administration's forceful response to the emplacement of Soviet ballistic missiles in Cuba in 1962.[12] The Soviet leadership did not count on the extent of American assistance to the Afghan resistance to their occupation of Afghanistan in 1979.[13] In dealing with the United States, Iraq's Saddam Hussein miscalculated twice—in 1991 and again in 2003—on the second occasion, fatally for himself.

These mistakes were not, or at least not entirely, the result of ignorance, negligence, or overconfidence. Before the events that galvanized the United States, the American public, and usually American policymakers as well, were not at all disposed to the courses of action that, after the events, they followed. Their responses came as a surprise to them as well as to their adversaries.[14]

The democratic features of its foreign policymaking have also, however, brought benefits to the United States. They have given other countries ways to gain access to American decisions that affect them.

This has enabled the American government to maintain reasonably cordial ties simultaneously with countries that are rivals: Arabs and Israelis, Greeks and Turks, Indians and Pakistanis have all found friends and advocates in the complicated, diverse machinery of American foreign policy. None has felt entirely excluded by the United States, a useful state of affairs for a country with the global interests that America came to have after World War II.

As for the inability to pursue a fixed design, America has indeed abandoned major projects because of public opposition to them—notably, the wars in Korea, Vietnam, and Iraq.[15] The stalemate in Korea and the failures in Vietnam and Iraq tarnished the American reputation for reliability and left the people of those countries (in Korea, the northern part) living under governments that did not, to say the least, embody American political values.

On the other hand, the United States did persevere in the three most important conflicts of the twentieth century. The coalition of which it was a part emerged victorious from the two world wars and the Cold War, in no small part because of American efforts.‡ Where the country did not persist, moreover, this may ultimately have worked to America's advantage. The public judged that continuing an American combat role in Korea, Vietnam, and Iraq would bring more costs than benefits, and while it is impossible to know what would have occurred had the United States persevered, that may well have been the correct judgment. The course of the three wars does illustrate inconstancy in American foreign policy; but another word for inconstancy is flexibility, and flexibility has advantages, just as firmness of purpose does. Flexibility can

---

‡ In fact, democracy can provide a broader, sturdier base for foreign policy than dictatorship. In January 1762, during the Seven Years' War, the death of the Russian Empress Elizabeth brought her son Paul to the throne. He abruptly changed Russian policy in the war, making peace with Prussia, which saved the political fortunes of the beleaguered Prussian King Frederick the Great. In April 1945, 183 years later, the American president Franklin D. Roosevelt died as World War II was still raging in Europe. Germany's Propaganda Minister, Josef Goebbels, was certain that history would repeat itself, that American policy would change, and Nazi Germany would be saved. Ian Kershaw, *Hitler 1936–1945: Nemesis*, New York: W.W. Norton & Company, 2000, pp. 791–792. No such thing happened. The United States being a democracy, Roosevelt's successor, Harry Truman, continued his predecessor's war policy, which aimed at, and the next month achieved, the unconditional surrender of Hitler's Germany.

assist in avoiding what economists call the "sunk cost fallacy," in which people persist in an expensive project because they have already invested a great deal in it in the past, not because it promises rewards in the future. Political leaders are prone to this kind of behavior: they continue policies they have launched, despite setbacks, in the hope of ultimate vindication.[16] The sovereignty of the public makes it possible, through elections, to replace such leaders with others without personally driven commitments, who can therefore more easily change course.

America's unusually democratic foreign policy has had other advantages historically. The country's democratic habits of cooperation, transparency, and respect for the sovereignty of other countries made the American-centered anti-communist coalition in the Cold War more effective and more durable than was the bloc controlled by the Soviet Union, which practiced none of those things.[17]

The democratic character of its foreign policy was never optional for the United States. The country was born a democracy, and democratic government was, in a sense, its reason for being. Nor did Americans choose their democratic political system with an eye toward maximizing their country's power and influence beyond its borders. As it turned out, however, this democratic foreign policy, while sometimes a liability, was at least as often an asset; and whatever the balance of geopolitical profit and loss from policymaking using multiple channels and in which public opinion ultimately reigns supreme, democracy did not prevent the United States of America from becoming, in the twentieth and twenty-first centuries, the most powerful country in the world.

INTRODUCTION

1. See, among many examples that could be cited, Louis Hartz, *The Liberal Tradition in America*, New York: Harcourt, Brace & World, 1955; James Kurth, *The American Way of Empire*, Washington, DC: Washington Books, 2019, p. 83; Robert Kagan, *Dangerous Nation: America and the World, 1600–1898*, London: Atlantic Books, 2006, p. 16; and George C. Herring, *From Colony to Empire: U.S. Foreign Relations Since 1776*, New York: Oxford University Press, 2008, p. 3.

2. *Webster's Encyclopedic Unabridged Dictionary of the English Language*, New York: Portland House, 1989, p. 707 defines ideology as "the body of doctrine … of a social movement, class, or large group" and "a body of doctrine with reference to some political and cultural plan."

3. See David Cannadine, *Victorious Century: The United Kingdom, 1800–1906*, New York: Penguin Books, 2019, pp. 376–377.

4. See pp. 12, 38, 52.

5. See Michael Mandelbaum, *The Four Ages of American Foreign Policy: Weak Power, Great Power, Superpower, Hyperpower*, New York: Oxford University Press, 2022, pp. 65–66, 148–150.

6. *Ibid.*, pp. 133–139.

7. See Arthur M. Schlesinger, Jr., *The Imperial Presidency*, Boston: Houghton Mifflin Company, 1973.

8. Mandelbaum, *op. cit.*, passim.

CHAPTER 1

1. Quoted in Robert Kagan, *Dangerous Nation: America and the World, 1600–1898*, London: Atlantic Books, 2006, p. 37.

2. Quoted in Walter A. McDougall, *Throes of Democracy: The American Civil War Era, 1829–1877*, New York: HarperCollins, 2008, p. 378.

3. See Michael Mandelbaum, *Democracy's Good Name: The Rise and Risks of the World's Most Popular Form of Government*, New York: PublicAffairs, 2007, Chapter 1.

4. Michael Mandelbaum, *The Four Ages of American Foreign Policy: Weak Power, Great Power, Superpower, Hyperpower*, New York: Oxford University Press, 2022, p. 403. See also Michael Mandelbaum, *Mission Failure: America and the World in the Post-Cold War Era*, New York: Oxford University Press, 2016, pp. 11–12, 165–171, 372–375.

5. Michael Mandelbaum, *The Rise and Fall of Peace on Earth*, New York: Oxford University Press, 2019, pp. 1–3.

6. Robert E. Osgood, *Ideals and Self-Interest in America's Foreign Relations: The Great Transformation of the Twentieth Century*, Chicago: University of Chicago Press, 1953, pp. 333, 337.

7. Dexter Perkins, *The American Approach to Foreign Policy*, Revised Edition, New York: Atheneum, 1968, p. 117.

8. Quoted in George C. Herring, *From Colony to Superpower: U.S. Foreign Relations Since 1776*, New York: Oxford University Press, 2008, p. 12.

9. Walter A. McDougall, *Freedom Just Around the Corner: A New American History, 1585-1828*, New York: HarperCollins, 2004, pp. 45, 69, 112; Robert Middlekauff, *The Glorious Cause: The American Revolution, 1763–1789*, New York: Oxford University Press, 2005, pp. 244–245.

10. Quoted in McDougall, *Freedom Just Around the Corner*, p. 243.

11. Quoted in *ibid.*, p. 251.

12. On the different schools of historical explanation for the American Revolution, see *ibid.*, pp. 207–209.

13. Kagan, *op. cit.*, p. 153. "American nationalism has been defined in political rather than organic terms." Samuel P. Huntington, *American Politics: The Promise of Disharmony*, Cambridge, Massachusetts: The Belknap Press of Harvard University Press, 1981, p. 23.

14. Mandelbaum, *The Four Ages of American Foreign Policy*, p. 124.

15. "[T]he effects of Biblical religion, filtered through the lenses of American consciences and projected onto law, society, and politics … seem kaleidoscopic." McDougall, *Freedom Just Around the Corner*, p. xv.

16. Quoted in Kagan, *op. cit.*, p. 155.

17. James Kurth, *The American Way of Empire*, Washington, DC: Washington Books, 2019, pp. 58–60.

18. "By 1815 America had become the most evangelically Christian nation in the world." Gordon S. Wood, *Empire of Liberty: A History of the Early Republic, 1789-1815*, New York: Oxford University Press, 2009, p. 3.

19. Walter A. McDougall, *The Tragedy of U.S. Foreign Policy: How America's Civil Religion Betrayed the National Interest*, New Haven: Yale University Press, 2016, pp. 120–122.

20. Quoted in Charles A. Kupchan, *Isolationism: A History of America's Efforts to Shield Itself from the* World, New York: Oxford University Press, 2020, p. 37.

21. See *ibid.*, *passim*.

22. Kagan, *op. cit.*, pp. 160–165.

23. Herring, *op. cit.*, pp. 135–136, 154; Kupchan, *op. cit.*, pp. 110–111.

24. Herring, *op. cit.*, p. 216; Kagan, *op. cit.*, p. 156.

25. Herring, *op. cit.*, p. 216; Kagan, *op. cit.*, p. 255; Perkins, *op. cit.*, p. 142.

26. Kagan, *op. cit.*, pp. 286–288; McDougall, *The Tragedy of U.S. Foreign Policy*, p. 96.

27. See Chapter 2.

28. Thomas Jefferson to the Citizens of Washington, DC, 4 March 1809, https://founders.archives.gov/documents/Jefferson/03-01-02-0006

29. James T. Patterson, *Restless Giant: The United States from Watergate to Bush v. Gore*, New York, Oxford University Press, 2007, p. 152. Patterson notes that, more than three hundred years later, President Ronald Reagan liked to quote this phrase.

30. "When Jefferson learned early in 1800 of Napoleon's coup d'etat of November 1799 that overthrew the French Republic, he did not draw the lesson the Federalists did: that too much democracy led to dictatorship. Instead, he said, 'I read it as a lesson against standing armies.'" Wood, *op. cit.*, p. 292.

31. Quoted in Kupchan, *op. cit.*, p. 51. Alexander Hamilton made the same point: "Safety from external danger is the most powerful director of national conduct. Even the ardent love of liberty will, after a time, give way to its dictates … The continued effort and alarm attendant on a state or continual danger will compel nations the most attached to liberty, to resort for repose and security, to institutions which have a tendency to destroy their civil and political rights." Quoted in Aaron Friedberg, *In the Shadow of the Garrison State: America's Anti-Statism and Its Cold War Grand Strategy*, Princeton: Princeton University Press, 2000, p. 12.

32. Quoted in Robert Kagan, *The Ghost at the Feast: America and the Collapse of World Order, 1900–1941*, New York: Alfred A. Knopf, 2023, p. 178.

33. Quoted in Kupchan, *op. cit.*, p. 294.

34. McDougall, *Freedom Just Around the Corner*, p. 362.

35. James Alan McPherson, *Battle Cry of Freedom: The Civil War Era*, New York: Oxford University Press, 1988, pp. 287–288.

36. David M. Kennedy, *Freedom from Fear: The American People in Depression and War, 1929–1945*, New York: Oxford University Press, 1999, pp. 748–760.

37. A previous "Red Scare" had taken place immediately after World War I, which involved arrests and deportations. According to one historian, "Not for at least half a century, perhaps at no time in our history, had there been such a wholesale violation of civil liberties." William E. Leuchtenberg, *The Perils of Prosperity, 1914–32*, Chicago: University of Chicago Press, 1993, p. 78.

38. James M. Patterson, *Grand Expectations: The United States, 1945–1974*, New York: Oxford University Press, 1996, pp. 178–193, 236–242.

39. Mandelbaum, *Mission Failure*, pp. 154–158.

40. See Mandelbaum, *The Four Ages of American Foreign Policy*, pp. 108–110.

41. McDougall, *Throes of Democracy*, p. 379; Mandelbaum, *The Four Ages of American Foreign Policy*, p. 101. Lincoln said that if the South succeeded in leaving the Union, "the hopes of the friends of freedom throughout the world would be destroyed … Our example for more than eighty years would not only be lost, but it would be quoted as a conclusive proof that man is unfit for self-government." Quoted in McPherson, *op. cit.*, p. 246.

42. See Tony Smith, *America's Mission: The United States and the Worldwide Struggle for Democracy in the Twentieth Century*, Princeton: Princeton University Press,

1994, pp. 19–28; Mandelbaum, *The Four Ages of American Foreign Policy*, pp. 110–111; Kagan, *Dangerous Nation*, pp. 270–273.

43. On the history of Reconstruction, see Richard D. White, *The Republic for Which It Stands: The United States During Reconstruction and the Gilded Age, 1865–1896*, New York: Oxford University Press, 2017, Chapter 1, Chapter 2, and pp. 332–336.

44. Kagan, *Dangerous Nation*, pp. 391–394, 406–408. "Three factors led to the war in Cuba: the century-long interest in a nearby island, American economic ties there, and public concern about a brutal, extensively reported war in the neighborhood." Mandelbaum, *The Four Ages of American Foreign Policy*, p. 143.

45. Kagan, *The Ghost at the Feast*, pp. 53–61; Walter A. McDougall, *Promised Land, Crusader State: The American Encounter with the World Since 1776*, Boston: Houghton Mifflin, 1997, pp. 113–114.

46. Charles S. Maier, *Among Empires: American Ascendancy and Its Predecessors*, Cambridge, Massachusetts: Harvard University Press, 2006, p. 68.

47. "For all efforts to pin it down, the term *empire* still courts multiple confusions." Maier, *op. cit.*, p. 40.

48. Empires are "relationships of political control imposed by some political societies over the effective sovereignty of other political societies." Michael Doyle, *Empires*, Ithaca: Cornell University Press, 1986, p. 19.

49. Herring, *op. cit.*, p. 102.

50. *Ibid.*, p. 337.

51. Independence might have come sooner but for the two world wars.

52. Mandelbaum, *The Four Ages of American Foreign Policy*, pp. 145–146.

53. One historian refers to "major programs of ethnic cleansing in the South and West from early settlement through the nineteenth century." Maier, *op. cit.*, p. 29.

54. Kagan, *Dangerous Nation*, p. 131.

55. Mandelbaum, *The Four Ages of American Foreign Policy*, pp. 87–89.

56. Kurth, *op. cit.*, p. 32.

57. "Chronic wrongdoing, or an impotence which results in a general loosening of the ties of civilized society, may in America, as elsewhere, ultimately require intervention by some civilized nation, and in the Western Hemisphere the adherence of the United States to the Monroe Doctrine may force the United States, however reluctantly, in flagrant cases of such wrongdoing or impotence, to the exercise of an international police power." Quoted in Kupchan, *op. cit.*, p. 207.

58. Elihu Root, secretary of state in the administrations of William McKinley and Theodore Roosevelt, said of these interventions: "First. We do not want to take them for ourselves. Second. We do not want any foreign nations to take them for themselves. Third. We want to help them." Quoted in Kagan, *The Ghost at the Feast*, p. 71.

59. Perkins, *op. cit.*, pp. 42–43.

60. Michael Mandelbaum, *The Ideas That Conquered the World: Peace, Democracy, and Free Markets in the Twenty-First Century*, New York: PublicAffairs, 2002, p. 63. See also Maier, *op. cit.*, p. 62–63.

61. Maier, *op. cit.*, p. 7.

62. Perkins, *op. cit.*, pp. 126–127.

63.   Osgood, *op. cit.*, pp. 68–70; Herring, *op. cit.*, pp. 360–363; Mandelbaum, *The Four Ages of American Foreign Policy*, pp. 151–152.

64.   Daniel Kurtz-Phelan, *The China Mission: George Marshall's Unfinished War*, New York: Alfred A. Knopf, 2018.

65.   Mandelbaum, *The Four Ages of American Foreign Policy*, pp. 333–335; Mandelbaum, *Mission Failure*, pp. 250–272.

66.   Mandelbaum, *The Four Ages of American Foreign Policy*, p. 178.

67.   On Thomas Jefferson's ideological approach to foreign policy, see Robert W. Tucker and David C. Hendrickson, *Empire of Liberty: The Statecraft of Thomas Jefferson*, New York: Oxford University Press, 1990.

68.   Leuchtenberg, *op. cit.*, p. 2.

69.   Mandelbaum, *The Four Ages of American Foreign Policy*, p. 159.

70.   Osgood, *op. cit.*, Chapter 6; Kagan, *The Ghost at the Feast*, pp. 105, 163.

71.   On the impact on American public opinion of the most dramatic sinking of the passenger liner *Lusitania*, see p. 112.

72.   Osgood, *op. cit.*, p. 223.

73.   The United States, he said, would "fight for the things which we have always carried nearest our hearts—for democracy, for the right of those who submit to authority to have a voice in their own governments, for the rights and liberties of small nations, for a universal dominion of right by such a concert of free peoples as shall bring peace and safety to all nations and make the world itself at last free." Quoted in Kagan, *The Ghost at the Feast*, p. 183.

74.   Mandelbaum, *The Four Ages of American Foreign Policy*, p. 166. The text of the Fourteen Points speech can be found at https://avalon.law.yale.edu/20th_century/wilson14.asp

75.   The proponents included prominent Republicans, such as Theodore Roosevelt. Kagan, *The Ghost at the Feast*, pp. 116, 230–232.

76.   Quoted in Margaret MacMillan, *Paris, 1919: Six Months That Changed the World*, New York: Random House, 2001, p. 32.

77.   The article read: "The Members of the League undertake to respect and preserve as against external aggression the territorial integrity and existing political independence of all Members of the League."

78.   McDougall, *Promised Land, Crusader State*, p. 142.

79.   *Ibid.*, p. 145.

80.   Mandelbaum, *The Four Ages of American Foreign Policy*, pp. 182–183.

81.   The Washington Treaties did have a precedent of sorts. In April 1817, in the wake of the War of 1812, the United States and Great Britain signed an agreement providing for naval disarmament on the Great Lakes. See Daniel Walker Howe, *What Hath God Wrought: The Transformation of America, 1815–1848*, New York: Oxford University Press, 2007, p. 96.

82.   Secretary of State Hughes said of the treaties, "We are taking perhaps the greatest forward step in history to establish the reign of peace." Quoted in Osgood, *op. cit.*, p. 342. On the popularity of the idea of disarmament in the United States at that time, see Herring, *op. cit.*, p. 452.

83.   Herring, *op. cit.*, p. 456.

84. For examples of Roosevelt's rhetoric to this effect, see David M. Kennedy, *Freedom from Fear: The American People in Depression and War, 1929-1945*, New York, Oxford University Press, 1999, p. 421, and Osgood, *op. cit.*, pp. 412 and 425.

85. In August 1941, the United States was effectively, if not officially, a belligerent in the naval war in the Atlantic and was providing Britain with armaments and other supplies on a large scale.

86. Mandelbaum, *The Four Ages of American Foreign Policy*, p. 202; Kennedy, *op. cit.*, p. 496.

87. Quoted in Mandelbaum, *The Four Ages of American Foreign Policy*, p. 257.

88. Quoted in Patterson, *op. cit.*, p. 279.

89. Michael Mandelbaum, *The Nuclear Question: The United States and Nuclear Weapons, 1946-1976*, New York: Cambridge University Press, 1979, Chapter 2.

90. The early arms control accords included the Strategic Arms Limitation agreements of 1972 and 1974 as well as a 1979 pact that was informally observed although never formally ratified by the United States. The 1972 accords included an effective ban on Anti-Ballistic Missile systems, which averted a potentially expensive competition in designing and building defensive systems. See Mandelbaum, *The Four Ages of American Foreign Policy*, pp. 317-319.

91. *Ibid.*, pp. 319-320.

92. Michael Mandelbaum, *The Dawn of Peace in Europe*, New York: The Twentieth Century Fund, 1996, Part II.

93. On détente, see Mandelbaum, *The Four Ages of American Foreign Policy*, pp. 313-325; and Herring, *op. cit.*, pp. 770-775.

94. Mandelbaum, *The Four Ages of American Foreign Policy*, pp. 323-324.

95. Patterson, *Restless Giant*, p. 102.

96. Another manifestation of foreign-policy realism by the Nixon administration came in for criticism. In 1971, the government of Pakistan brutally repressed opposition to it in what was then the eastern wing of the country and subsequently became independent Bangladesh. Because Pakistan was America's ally during the Cold War and was involved in the Nixon administration's then-secret outreach to China, the administration aligned itself with the Pakistani government despite its gross violation of human rights. This did not sit well with Americans who believed that the defense of individual rights should be a major part of American foreign policy. See Herring, *op. cit.*, pp. 788-790.

97. On this issue, see Daniel Pipes and Adam Garfinkle, editors, *Friendly Tyrants: An American Dilemma*, New York: St. Martin's Press, 1991.

98. Mandelbaum, *The Four Ages of American Foreign Policy*, pp. 340-341.

99. McDougall, *Promised Land, Crusader State*, pp. 190-194.

100. Communism in Europe collapsed in part because its leaders "did not defend it; and they did not defend it because, by virtue of its failures, they had come to believe—many of them, at least—that it was not worth defending." Mandelbaum, *The Four Ages of American Foreign Policy*, p. 373.

101.   "The Cold War involved the defense of the West; post-Cold War foreign policy aspired to the political and ideological extension of the West." Mandelbaum, *Mission Failure*, p. 5. An official of the Clinton administration said in 1993 that "the successor to a doctrine of [Cold War] containment must be a strategy of enlargement—enlargement of the world's community of market democracies," quoted p. 17.

102.   *Ibid.*, pp. 22–29.

103.   In the early nineteenth century, some American leaders were skeptical that all peoples, and especially Latin Americans, could manage stable democracies. Kupchan, *op. cit.*, pp. 109–111, 121. By the second half of the twentieth century, that skepticism had vanished.

104.   Mandelbaum, *Democracy's Good Name*, p. xi.

105.   Mandelbaum, *The Rise and Fall of Peace on Earth, passim*.

106.   On the failure of democracy in the Arab world, see Mandelbaum, *Mission Failure*, pp. 287–310.

107.   The initial post–Cold War humanitarian intervention took place in 1991 in the Kurdish region of Iraq in the wake of the American-led war to evict Iraqi forces from neighboring Kuwait, which they had invaded and occupied. *Ibid.*, pp. 3–4, 86–87.

108.   See p. 21.

109.   Rajan Menon, *The Conceit of Humanitarian Intervention*, New York: Oxford University Press, 2016, pp. 5–7.

110.   *Ibid.*, pp. 7, 44.

111.   *Ibid.*, p. 9.

112.   In early 2011, the United States used force—aerial bombardment—to displace the government of Libya but did not put troops on the ground and did not engage in hands-on state-building there. Mandelbaum, *Mission Failure*, pp. 301–302; Mandelbaum, *The Four Ages of American Foreign Policy*, p. 444.

113.   On Iraq, see Melvyn P. Leffler, *Confronting Saddam Hussein: George W. Bush and the Invasion of Iraq*, New York: Oxford University Press, 2023, Chapter 4.

114.   Mandelbaum, *Democracy's Good Name*, pp. 43–44; Mandelbaum, *Mission Failure*, pp. 131–132; Mandelbaum, *The Four Ages of American Foreign Policy*, pp. 431–432; Kurth, *op. cit.*, pp. 107–108.

115.   This is the subject of Mandelbaum, *The Rise and Fall of Peace on Earth*.

116.   Quoted in Hal Brands, "The Age of Amorality," *Foreign Affairs*, March/April 2024, p. 109.

117.   In its first six months, the second administration of Donald J. Trump also made American values a part of its foreign policy by criticizing governments that, it said, were violating principles in which it believed. The targets of its criticisms, however—the governments of Western Europe for restrictions on political parties at the right end of the political spectrum, and the government of South Africa for infringing on the rights of its white citizens—differed sharply from those at which the values-based criticisms of previous administrations had been directed. See Jason Willick, "The meaning behind Trump's foreign policy trolling," *The Washington Post*, June 3, 2025, https://www.washingtonpost.com/opinions/2025/06/03/trump-foreign-policy-realist-idealist

CHAPTER 2

1. C. Donald Johnson, *The Wealth of a Nation: A History of Trade Politics in America*, New York: Oxford University Press, 2018, pp. 11, 14, 16.

2. Adam Smith wrote his landmark economic treatise of 1776, *The Wealth of Nations*, as a polemic against the idea that a country's gold and silver constituted its wealth, arguing instead, as the world has come to accept in the quarter-millennium since the book's publication, that a nation's wealth in fact consists of the sum of all it produces. Johnson, *op. cit.*, pp. 11, 14, 16; Jeffry A. Frieden, *Global Capitalism: Its Fall and Rise in the Twentieth Century*, New York: Viking, 2006, p. 3. The mercantilist system had the effect of enriching some people at the expense of others. It worked to the disadvantage of those who depended on salaries, for example, because it often entailed measures to repress wages for the purpose of discouraging imports. Johnson, *op. cit.*, pp. 8, 10, 15, 16, 19.

3. The United States has, for example, imposed economic sanctions for the purpose of changing the domestic or foreign policies of other countries more frequently than have other countries. "Of the 116 cases [of economic sanctions since World War I] documented … the United States, either alone or in concert with its allies, has deployed sanctions 77 times." Gary Clyde Hufbauer, Jeffrey J. Schott, and Kimberly Ann Elliott, *Economic Sanctions Reconsidered: History and Current Policy*, Second Edition, Washington, DC: Institute for International Economics, 1990, pp. 8–9.

4. Walter A. McDougall, *Freedom Just Around the Corner: A New American History, 1585–1828*, New York: HarperCollins, 2004, pp. 115, 221; Douglas A. Irwin, *Clashing over Commerce: A History of US Trade Policy*, Chicago: University of Chicago Press, 2017, pp. 35–38.

5. Woodrow Wilson expressed this belief in 1919: "A nation that is boycotted is a nation that is in sight of surrender. Apply this economic, peaceful, silent, deadly remedy and there will be no need for force … it brings a pressure upon the nation which, in my judgment, no modern nation could resist." Quoted in Hufbauer et al., *op. cit.*, p. 9.

6. He actually said, "After all, the chief business of the American people is business. They are profoundly concerned with producing, buying, selling, investing and prospering in the world." Ellen Terrell, "When a Quote Is Not (Exactly) a Quote," Library of Congress Blogs: Inside Adams, June 17, 2019. https://blogs.loc.gov/inside_adams/2019/01/when-a-quote-is-not-exactly-a-quote-the-business-of-america-is-business-edition

7. Walter A. McDougall, *Throes of Democracy: The American Civil War Era, 1829–1877*, New York: HarperCollins, 2008, pp. xvi–xvii; McDougall, *Freedom Just Around the Corner*, pp. 124–125; Robert Kagan, *Dangerous Nation: America and the World, 1600–1898*, London: Atlantic Books, 2006, p. 6.

8. McDougall, *Freedom Just Around the Corner*, p. 220.

9. George C. Herring, *From Colony to Superpower: U.S. Foreign Relations Since 1776*, New York: Oxford University Press, 2008, p. 37.

10. The third major category of cross-border flows, that of people—that is, immigration—while important politically and economically in the history of the

United States, has never become a tool of foreign policy in the manner of trade and the provision of capital.

11. One definition of sanctions is "the deliberate, government-inspired withdrawal, or threat of withdrawal, of customary trade or financial relations." Hufbauer et al., *op. cit.*, p. 2.

12. In general, sanctions have three broad goals, which are not mutually exclusive: to coerce, to deter, and to punish. Richard Haass, "Conclusion: Lessons and Recommendations," in Richard Haass, editor, *Economic Sanctions and American Diplomacy*, New York: The Council on Foreign Relations, 1998, p. 199.

13. Hufbauer et al., *op. cit.*, pp. 3, 11.

14. *Ibid.*, p. 92.

15. "Sanctions create powerful incentives for evasion. It could be said that a sieve leaks like a sanction." *Ibid.*, p. 75.

16. See pp. 60–62.

17. Robert Middlekauff, *The Glorious Cause: The American Revolution, 1763–1789*, New York: Oxford University Press, Second Edition, 2005, pp. 120–121, 214; Michael Mandelbaum, *The Four Ages of American Foreign Policy: Weak Power, Great Power, Superpower, Hyperpower*, New York: Oxford University Press, 2022, pp. 17–18; Irwin, *op. cit.*, pp. 40–41.

18. McDougall, *Freedom Just Around the Corner*, p. 225; Johnson, *op. cit.*, p. 37.

19. This is a major theme of Robert W. Tucker and David C. Hendrickson, *The Fall of the First British Empire: Origins of the War of American Independence*, Baltimore: Johns Hopkins University Press, 1982.

20. Herring, *op. cit.*, p. 40; Johnson, *op. cit.*, pp. 38–39; Irwin, *op. cit.*, p. 53.

21. Kagan, *op. cit.*, pp. 96–97; Charles Kupchan, *Isolationism: A History of America's Efforts to Shield Itself from the World*, New York: Oxford University Press, 2020, p. 37.

22. On the embargo, see Tucker and Hendrickson, *op. cit.*, pp. 649–658, Herring, *op. cit.*, pp. 119–121, and Irwin, *op. cit.*, pp. 101–113.

23. Gordon S. Wood, *Empire of Liberty: A History of the Early Republic, 1789–1815*, New York: Oxford University Press, 2009, pp. 628–629.

24. McDougall, *Freedom Just Around the Corner*, p. 401.

25. Irwin, *op. cit.*, p. 106.

26. Wood, *op. cit.*, p. 647.

27. Johnson, *op. cit.*, Chapter 2.

28. Irwin, *op. cit.*, pp. 3, 10.

29. Daniel Walker Howe, *What Hath God Wrought: The Transformation of America, 1815–1848*, New York: Oxford University Press, 2007, p. 273; McDougall, *Throes of Democracy*, pp. 337–339.

30. James M. McPherson, *Battle Cry of Freedom: The Civil War Era*, New York: Oxford University Press, 1988, pp. 383–384; McDougall, *Throes of Democracy*, pp. 418–420; Herring, *op. cit.*, pp. 226–227.

31. "British imports of cotton from the South in 1862 amounted to about 3 percent of the 1860 total." McPherson, *op. cit.*, p. 384.

32. Herring, *op. cit.*, pp. 232–234; McPherson, *op. cit.*, pp. 384–385; McDougall, *Throes of Democracy*, p. 438.

33. McPherson, *op. cit.*, p. 311.

34. Frieden, *op. cit.*, pp. 39–42; Irwin, *op. cit.*, pp. 7, 322; McDougall, *Throes of Democracy*, p. 434.

35. "During the fiscal year ending on June 30, 1889, the tariff provided 60 percent of federal revenue." Richard White, *The Republic for Which It Stands: The United States During Reconstruction and the Gilded Age, 1865–1896*, New York: Oxford University Press, 2017, p. 631.

36. Kevin H. O'Rourke and Jeffrey G. Williamson, *Globalization and History: The Evolution of a Nineteenth-Century Atlantic Economy*, Cambridge, Massachusetts: MIT Press, 1999, pp. 35, 41; Frieden, *op. cit.*, p. 5.

37. Alan Greenspan and Adrian Wooldridge, *Capitalism in America: A History*, New York: Penguin Press, 2018, Chapter 3.

38. On Dollar Diplomacy, see Robert Kagan, *The Ghost at the Feast: America and the Collapse of the World Order, 1900–1941*, New York: Alfred A. Knopf, 2023, pp. 66, 74; Mandelbaum, *op. cit.*, p. 127; and Walter LaFeber, *The American Age: U.S. Foreign Policy at Home and Abroad, 1750 to the Present*, Second Edition, New York: W.W. Norton and Company, 1994, pp. 236, 258–262.

39. "Thanks to Allied war purchases, American per capita income during the period of neutrality [September 1914 to April 1917] rose by an astonishing 25 percent." Kagan, *The Ghost at the Feast*, p. 115.

40. William E. Leuchtenberg, *The Perils of Prosperity, 1914–1932*, Second Edition, Chicago: University of Chicago Press, 1993, p. 15; Herring, *op. cit.*, p. 401.

41. "Commerce with Germany and Austria fell from $169 million in 1914 to $1 million in 1916." Leuchtenberg, *op. cit.*, p. 14.

42. John Milton Cooper, *Woodrow Wilson: A Biography*, New York: Alfred A. Knopf, 2009, p. 285; Herring, *op. cit.*, p. 402.

43. Kagan, *The Ghost at the Feast*, p. 117.

44. Mandelbaum, *op. cit.*, p. 186.

45. David M. Kennedy, *Freedom from Fear: The American People in Depression and War, 1929–1945*, New York: Oxford University Press, 1999, pp. 34, 72; Kagan, *The Ghost at the Feast*, pp. 269, 277.

46. Frieden, *op. cit.*, pp. 144–145; Herring, *op. cit.*, p. 462; Leuchtenberg, *op. cit.*, p. 109.

47. Mandelbaum, *op. cit.*, p. 187; Herring, *op. cit.*, p. 459.

48. "The economic collapse of 1929–1934 was unprecedented in its depth and breadth. There had been cyclical crises before, but never like this. The economies of the industrialized world disintegrated for five years and more, as output dropped by one-fifth and unemployment went above one-quarter of the labor force almost everywhere." Frieden, *op. cit.*, p. 173. See also Irwin, *op. cit.*, p. 386.

49. This is the theme of Charles Kindleberger, *The World in Depression, 1929–1939*, Berkeley: University of California Press, 1973. See also James Kurth, *The American Way of Empire: How American Won a World—But Lost Her Way*, Washington, DC: Potomac Books, 2019, pp. 201–202 and Charles S. Maier, *Among Empires: American Ascendancy and Its Predecessors*, Cambridge, Massachusetts: Harvard University Press, 2006, pp. 207–208.

50. Kennedy, *op. cit.*, pp. 155–157; Johnson, *op. cit.*, pp. 246–247.

51.   Irwin, *op. cit.*, p. 396.

52.   Kennedy, *op. cit.*, p. 505.

53.   Walter LaFeber, *The Clash: U.S.-Japanese Relations Throughout History*, New York: W.W. Norton and Company, 1997, pp. 189, 193.

54.   As has also often been the case, the sanctioned country sought alternative sources of supply of what it was being denied. For Japan the alternative source of oil was in Southeast Asia, which it proceeded to conquer.

55.   Robert Dallek, *Franklin D. Roosevelt and American Foreign Policy, 1932–1945*, New York: Oxford University Press, 1979, p. 269; Kennedy, *op. cit.*, p. 510.

56.   LaFeber, *The Clash*, p. 194.

57.   *Ibid.*, p. 200; Dallek, *op. cit.*, pp. 274, 302; Kennedy, *op. cit.*, p. 511.

58.   Johnson, *op. cit.*, pp. 287–288; Kupchan, *op. cit.*, pp. 282–285.

59.   On eighteenth-century British foreign policy, see Brendan Simms, *Three Victories and a Defeat: The Rise and Fall of the First British Empire, 1714–1783*, New York: Basic Books, 2007.

60.   The last word of the phrase misleads in that, while two of the three members of the winning coalition, the United States and Great Britain, had democratic governments, the Soviet Union certainly did not.

61.   "[I]n a long-drawn-out Great Power (and usually coalition) war, victory has repeatedly gone to the side with the more flourishing productive base—or, as the Spanish captains used to say, to him who has the last escudo." Paul Kennedy, *The Rise and Fall of the Great Powers: Economic Change and Military Conflict from 1500 to 200*, New York: Random House, 1988, p. xxiv.

62.   Frieden, *op. cit.*, pp. 261–262.

63.   Irwin, *op. cit.*, p. 455.

64.   In addressing the Bretton Woods Conference, the American Secretary of the Treasury Henry Morgenthau spoke of "the roles of collapsing trade and currency disorder in paving the path to war in the 1930s." Benn Steil, *The Battle of Bretton Woods: John Maynard Keynes, Harry Dexter White, and the Making of a New World Order*, Princeton: Princeton University Press, 2013, p. 13. See also Benn Steil, *The Marshall Plan: Dawn of the Cold War*, New York: Simon & Schuster, 2018, p. 14.

65.   In 1946, the United States made an emergency loan to Great Britain that was justified on strategic as well as economic and humanitarian grounds. Herring, *op. cit.*, pp. 605–606; Frieden, *op. cit.*, p. 266; Johnson, *op. cit.*, p. 338.

66.   Quoted in Mandelbaum, *op. cit.*, pp. 257–258.

67.   Johnson, *op. cit.*, p. 354.

68.   "Food was no longer reaching the cities from the country; factories were scrounging for vital raw materials. Gold and dollars with which to import essentials such as fuel were nearly evaporated. Strikes were spreading. Inflation was mounting." Steil, *The Marshall Plan*, p. 94.

69.   James T. Patterson, *Grand Expectations: The United States, 1945–1974*, New York: Oxford University Press, 1996, p. 130; Mandelbaum, *op. cit.*, p. 259; Steil, *The Marshall Plan*, p. 102.

70.   Herring, *op. cit.*, p. 620. "[T]he United States provided 1 to 2 percent of its GNP [gross national product] in aid from 1945 through the early 1950s, first

in emergency postwar relief to war-stricken countries, then from 1948 through 1951 in Marshall Plan assistance, and thereafter in military aid." Maier, *op. cit.*, p. 213.

71.   The Marshall Plan had a specific economic purpose. European countries suffered from a "dollar gap." They lacked the dollars required for needed purchases from the United States. Marshall funds filled that gap. Irwin, *op. cit.*, p. 496. "A majority of the Marshall Plan funds were spent on food, fuel, and raw materials that relieved the resource constraints at the time, not on investments or infrastructure." *Ibid.*, p. 497. See also Steil, *The Marshall Plan*, p. 166.

72.   Steil, *The Marshall Plan*, p. 136.

73.   Patterson, *op. cit.*, p. 131.

74.   Kurth, *op. cit.*, p. 28.

75.   "United States military procurement pumped $2.3 billion into a lagging Japanese economy. Exports soared to 50 percent above prewar levels; the GNP increased by 10 percent." Herring, *op. cit.*, p. 646.

76.   Johnson, *op. cit.*, p. 439.

77.   Irwin, *op. cit.*, p. 22.

78.   LaFeber, *The Clash*, p. 179; Frieden, *op. cit.*, p. 248.

79.   Mandelbaum, *op. cit.*, p. 194.

80.   Irwin, *op. cit.*, pp. 492–495; Frieden, *op. cit.*, p. 255.

81.   Reversing the trade policy it had carried out after World War I, in the wake of World War II the United States opened its markets to make it possible for Europe, and ultimately the rest of the world, to earn dollars by exporting to the American market. They could use the dollars they earned to pay for American products.

82.   In this usage, the First World was the American-led West, the Second World was the Soviet-led Communist bloc.

83.   Herring, *op. cit.*, pp. 716–718.

84.   Frieden, *op. cit.*, p. 292.

85.   See pp. 14, 25, 43–45, 50–51.

86.   Mandelbaum, *op. cit.*, p. 247.

87.   In response to Afghanistan, among other measures the United States stopped the sale of American grain to the Soviet Union. On the occasion of the crackdown in Poland, America tried, ultimately unsuccessfully, to halt the building of a pipeline to carry natural gas from Siberia in the Soviet Union to Western Europe. Herring, *op. cit.*, p. 854; Hufbauer et al., *op. cit.*, pp. 1, 82.

88.   Susan Kaufman Purcell, "Cuba," in Haass, editor, *op. cit.*

89.   Cuba had 7.1 million people in 1960 and 11.4 million in 2022.

90.   "Economic sanctions seem most effective when aimed against erstwhile friends and close trading partners. In contrast, sanctions directed against target countries that have long been adversaries of the sender countries, or against targets that have little trade with the sender country, are generally less successful." Hufbauer et al., *op. cit.*, p. 99.

91.   *Ibid.*, pp. 5, 64; Herring, *op. cit.*, p. 676. Washington also imposed sanctions, in the form of restrictions on the amount of sugar it could sell in the United States, on the Dominican Republic—a small, ostensibly friendly country—in an effort

to compel the resident dictator there, Rafael Trujillo, to give up power. Hufbauer, *op. cit.*, p. 74. Trujillo was assassinated by the Dominican military in 1961.

92. Hufbauer et al., *op. cit.*, p. 7.

93. Mandelbaum, *op. cit.*, p. 316.

94. Johnson, *op. cit.*, p. 479. See also Chapter 1, pp. 42–43.

95. Specifically, the two oil shocks in that decade helped to bring about inflation and low economic growth. Mandelbaum, *op. cit.*, pp. 339–340.

96. See p. 45.

97. Mandelbaum, *op. cit.*, pp. 355–360. "The causes of the ultimate victory of the United States over the Soviet Union in the Cold War were many. It is clear, however, that among the central causes were the dynamism of the open international economy, the inability of the Soviet system to cope with this, and the pressures that this put upon the Soviet leadership to change—and ultimately to abandon—that system." Kurth, *op. cit.*, p. 148.

98. The loss of confidence took place principally in the Soviet Union. The countries of Eastern Europe, where communism had been imposed by the Red Army after 1945, had had far less confidence to begin with and soon lost whatever they had. Soviet military power kept the communist regimes of Eastern Europe in place. When that power ceased to be available to support them, those regimes collapsed.

99. Mandelbaum, *op. cit.*, p. 372.

100. "Once Sino-American relations had been concerned solely with matters of power—that is, with America's interests. After [the crackdown] by contrast, the political values and political practices of the two countries entered the picture. American policy toward China ceased to be based exclusively on the Chinese government's policies toward the Soviet Union and took into account that government's policies toward its own people." Michael Mandelbaum, *Mission Failure: America and the World in the Post–Cold War Era*, New York: Oxford University Press, 2016, p. 22. The administration of President George H.W. Bush, which was in office when the crackdown took place, reacted by suspending arms sales to China. The United States also threatened to penalize China for selling ballistic missiles to other countries in violation of an international agreement called the Missile Technology Control Regime. Robert Ross, "China," in Haass, editor, *op. cit.*, pp. 21–26.

101. Ross, in Haass, editor, *op. cit.*, p. 13.

102. The United States had had sanctions in place against Iran since the Iranian revolution of 1979. Patrick Clawson, "Iran," in Haass, editor, *op. cit.*, p. 85.

103. Mandelbaum, *The Four Ages of American Foreign Policy*, pp. 451–453.

104. Mandelbaum, *Mission Failure*, pp. 46–47.

105. Mandelbaum, *The Four Ages of American Foreign Policy*, p. 396; Paul Blustein, *The Chastening: Inside the Crisis that Rocked the Global Financial System and Humbled the IMF*, New York: PublicAffairs, 2001, pp. 228, 232.

106. Mandelbaum, *The Four Ages of American Foreign Policy*, p. 379.

107. Michael Mandelbaum, *Democracy's Good Name: The Rise and Risks of the World's Most Popular Form of Government*, New York: PublicAffairs, 2007, Chapter 3. President Bill Clinton declared that "By expanding trade we can advance the

cause of freedom and democracy around the world." Quoted in Mandelbaum, *The Four Ages of American Foreign Policy*, p. 392.

108. Kupchan, *op. cit.*, p. 325.

109. Walter A. McDougall, *Promised Land, Crusader State: The American Encounter with the World Since 1776*, Boston: Houghton Mifflin, 1997, p. 22; Wood, *op. cit.*, p. 189; Mandelbaum, *The Four Ages of American Foreign Policy*, p. 49.

110. Michael Howard, *The Invention of Peace: Reflections on War and International Order*, London: Profile Books, 2000, pp. 43–44. The American founders believed this too. Wood, *op. cit.*, p. 190; Kupchan, *op. cit.*, p. 68.

111. Mandelbaum, *Democracy's Good Name*, Chapter 4.

112. Mandelbaum, *The Four Ages of American Foreign Policy*, p. 412.

113. Ross, *op. cit.*, pp. 13, 17–18. "Once, American presidents talked of shaping China's rise. Boldly, they predicted that a growing middle class would surely start to demand individual freedoms, or at least a greater say in the running of their one-party state." Chaguan, "Defanging the Chinese tiger," *The Economist*, April 1, 2023, p. 34.

114. Irwin, *op. cit.*, pp. 672, 676; Herring, *op. cit.*, p. 937.

115. NAFTA, in particular, had an important political aim: to improve the historically uneasy relationship between the United States and its southern neighbor, Mexico.

116. "The Uruguay Round was the most ambitious and far-reaching multinational trade negotiation since the establishment of the GATT in 1947." Irwin, *op. cit.*, p. 651.

117. Mandelbaum, *The Four Ages of American Foreign Policy*, pp. 435–440.

118. Irwin, *op. cit.*, p. 686. At the beginning of Trump's second (nonconsecutive) presidential term, he imposed across-the-board tariffs. Insofar as their aim was clear, they were not levied for political but rather for economic purposes: to protect American industries and jobs. In that way Trump was emulating the Republican party's tariff policy between the Civil War and the New Deal.

119. Mandelbaum, *Mission Failure*, p. 37.

120. Henry Farrell and Abraham Newman, *Underground Empire: How America Weaponized the World Economy*, New York: Henry Holt, 2023, Chapter 3.

121. "In a speech in September [2022] Jake Sullivan, America's national security adviser, explained that the government wanted to hobble China's capabilities in 'foundational technologies,' such as artificial intelligence, biotech, and clean energy, to allow America to maintain as much of an edge as possible in these areas." "A daunting arsenal," *The Economist*, April 1, 2023, p. 14. Advanced chips are crucial to all these technologies, particularly artificial intelligence, which seemed destined to play a major role in twenty-first-century warfare.

122. On American policies designed to limit Chinese power, see Edward Fishman, *Chokepoints: American Power in the Age of Economic Warfare*, New York: Profile/Penguin, 2025, Part Four.

123. An overview of the American economic response to the Russian invasion of Ukraine is in *ibid.*, Part Five.

124. This is a major theme of Farrell and Newman, *op. cit.* See especially Chapter 2.

125. Wally Adeyemo, "America's New Sanctions Strategy: How Washington Can Stop the Russian War Machine and Strengthen the International Economic Order," *Foreign Affairs*, December 16, 2022, https://www.foreignaffairs.com/russian-federation/americas-new-sanctions-strategy. Because the global price of oil rose, Russian revenues remained high for the first two years of the war.

CHAPTER 3

1. See, for example, Dexter Perkins, *The American Approach to Foreign Policy*, New York: Atheneum, 1968, pp. 73–74.
2. See p. 8.
3. See pp. 8–9.
4. In *The Federalist Papers*, John Jay makes this point. See Perkins, *op. cit.*, pp. 157–158.
5. James T. Patterson, *Grand Expectations: The United States, 1945–1974*, New York: Oxford University Press, 1996, p. 213; Michael Mandelbaum, *The Four Ages of American Foreign Policy: Weak Power, Great Power, Superpower, Hyperpower*, New York: Oxford University Press, 2022, p. 275.
6. Aaron Wildavsky, "The Two Presidencies," *Trans-Action*, 4 (2), December, 1966.
7. Arthur M. Schlesinger, Jr., *The Imperial Presidency*, Boston: Houghton Mifflin, 1973.
8. In the Mexican War, Polk "successfully discovered the latent constitutional powers of the commander in chief to provoke a war, secure congressional support for it, shape the strategy for fighting it, appoint generals, and define the terms of peace. He probably did as much as anyone to expand the powers of the presidency." Daniel Walker Howe, *What Hath God Wrought: The Transformation of America, 1815–1848*, New York: Oxford University Press, 2007, p. 808. Debates about presidential authority in foreign policy go back to the beginning of the republic. See Gordon S. Wood, *Empire of Liberty: A History of the Early Republic, 1789–1815*, New York: Oxford University Press, 2009, pp. 184–185.
9. James T. Patterson, *Restless Giant: The United States from Watergate to Bush v. Gore*, New York: Oxford University Press, 2005, p. 233; Michael Mandelbaum, *Mission Failure: America and the World in the Post–Cold War Era*, New York: Oxford University Press, 2016, p. 190.
10. On this point, see Walter Russell Mead, *Special Providence: American Foreign Policy and How It Changed the World*, New York: Alfred A. Knopf, 2001, p. 40.
11. Quoted in Wood, *op. cit.*, p. 309. According to Wood, "In no country in the world did public opinion become more awesome and powerful than it did in increasingly democratic America." *Ibid.*, p. 312. One of Madison's successors as president, Abraham Lincoln, made the point this way: "Public sentiment is everything … *With* it, nothing can fail; *against* it, nothing can succeed." Quoted in Walter A. McDougall, *Throes of Democracy: The American Civil War Era 1929–1877*, New York: HarperCollins, 2008, p. 473.
12. The important American wars, each mentioned more than once in this chapter (and also listed on p. 12), are the Revolutionary War, the War of 1812, the Mexican War, the Civil War, the Spanish–American War, World War I, World War II, the Korean War, the Vietnam War, the Persian Gulf War of 1991, the Afghan War

that began in 2002, and the Iraq War (sometimes called the second Gulf War) of 2003.

13. Arthur F. Bentley's *The Process of Government*, published in 1908, is the founding text of this school of analysis.

14. See pp. 100–102.

15. Wood, *op. cit.*, pp. 185–187; George C. Herring, *From Colony to Superpower: U.S. Foreign Relations Since 1776*, New York: Oxford University Press, 2008, pp. 70–73.

16. Mandelbaum, *The Four Ages of American Foreign Policy*, p. 162; Robert Kagan, *The Ghost at the Feast: America and the Collapse of World Order, 1900–1941*, New York: Alfred A. Knopf, 2023, pp. 174–176; Robert Endicott Osgood, *Ideals and Self-Interest in America's Foreign Relations*, Chicago: University of Chicago Press, 1953, pp. 254–255.

17. Lynne Olson, *Those Angry Days: Roosevelt, Lindbergh, and America's Fight over World War II, 1939–1941*, New York: Random House Trade Paperback, 2013, pp. 51–52.

18. The term comes from the practice of nineteenth-century advocates of particular causes of gathering in the lobbies of public buildings or in hotels to try to convince officials to support their causes. It is often associated with the Willard Hotel in Washington, DC.

19. John Pomfret, *The Beautiful Country and the Middle Kingdom: America and China, 1776 to the Present*, New York: Henry Holt, 2016, p. 374; Herring, *op. cit.*, p. 579; Patterson, *Grand Expectations*, pp. 171–172.

20. Mandelbaum, *The Four Ages of American Foreign Policy*, p. 284.

21. For the argument that without the deeply anti-statist political tradition in the United States the components of the military-industrial complex might have been larger and more powerful than they actually were, see Aaron L. Friedberg, *In the Shadow of the Garrison State: America's Anti-Statism and Its Cold War Grand Strategy*, Princeton: Princeton University Press, 2000.

22. Herring, *op. cit.*, p. 399; Mandelbaum, *The Four Ages of American Foreign Policy*, p. 123; Kagan, *op. cit.*, pp. 90, 107–108, 172; David M. Kennedy, *Freedom from Fear: The American People in Depression and War, 1929–1945*, New York: Oxford University Press, 1999, p. 472.

23. Mandelbaum, *Mission Failure*, p. 71.

24. See, for example, John Mearsheimer and Stephen Walt, *The Israel Lobby and American Foreign Policy*, New York: Farrar, Straus and Giroux, 2007.

25. Robert Kagan, *Dangerous Nation: America and the World, 1600–1898*, London: Atlantic Books, 2006, pp. 286–289; Herring, *op. cit.*, pp. 285, 351–352.

26. America has "the oldest and third oldest political parties in the world, with the Democratic Party dating from the 1832 national convention that nominated Andrew Jackson for a second term and the Republican Party dating from 1854 protests against the Kansas-Nebraska Act allowing slavery in the territories." Michael Barone, *How America's Political Parties Change (and How They Don't)*, New York: Encounter Books, 2019, p. 2.

27. *Ibid.*, pp. 3–4.

28. In the third decade of the twenty-first century, the Democrats had become a coalition of the affluent and highly educated, racial minorities, and the very poor,

while the Republican coalition included rural dwellers, members of the white working class, and the religiously observant.

29. In the third decade of the twenty-first century, the major parties showed signs of trading places once again, with the Democrats in favor of engagement in international security affairs and the Republicans increasingly averse to it.

30. "It appears that the American public's natural tendency with regard to international issues is to pay them little heed." John E. Mueller, *War and Ideas: Selected Essays*, New York: Routledge, 2011, p. 166.

31. John Mueller, *War, Presidents, and Public Opinion*, New York: John Wiley & Sons, 1973, p. 154.

32. "[M]any people use their party identification as a shortcut method for arriving at a position on an issue. Rather than sort through the intricacies of argument on the issue, they prefer to take as cues the word of the leadership of their party. It is their method for minimizing information costs." *Ibid.*, p. 116.

33. Herring, *op. cit.*, p. 427.

34. Wood, *op. cit.*, pp. 188, 204; Walter A. McDougall, *Freedom Just Around the Corner: A New American History 1585–1828*, New York: HarperCollins, 2004, p. 321; Walter A. McDougall, *Promised Land, Crusader State: The American Encounter with the World Since 1776*, Boston: Houghton Mifflin, 1997, p. 29.

35. Charles A. Kupchan, *Isolationism: A History of America's Efforts to Shield Itself from the World*, New York: Oxford University Press, 2020, p. 97.

36. Wood, *op. cit.*, pp. 661–662.

37. See p. 120.

38. Mandelbaum, *The Four Ages of American Foreign Policy*, p. 71.

39. *Ibid.*, pp. 72–73.

40. Wood, *op. cit.*, p. 696.

41. Howe, *op. cit.*, p. 762.

42. Herring, *op. cit.*, p. 204.

43. James M. McPherson, *Battle Cry of Freedom: The Civil War Era*, New York: Oxford University Press, 1988, p. 47; Howe, *op. cit.*, pp. 742–743.

44. Howe, *op. cit.*, p. 770.

45. McPherson, *op. cit.*, pp. 506, 594.

46. *Ibid.*, pp. 775–776.

47. William Widenor, *Henry Cabot Lodge and the Search for an American Foreign Policy*, Berkeley: University of California Press, 1980, pp. 301, 309–310, 321; William E. Leuchtenberg, *The Perils of Prosperity, 1914–1932*, Second Edition, Chicago: University of Chicago Press, 1993, p. 58.

48. Kennedy, *op. cit.*, pp. 457–459. Secretary of the navy was then a more important post than it later became. Franklin Roosevelt himself had served as assistant secretary of the navy during World War I.

49. Herring, *op. cit.*, p. 704; Mandelbaum, *The Four Ages of American Foreign Policy*, p. 345.

50. "[T]he partisan divide on Iraq is considerably greater than on any military action over the last half century." Mueller, *War and Ideas*, p. 205.

51. See p. 82.

52. About the impact of Pearl Harbor on the American public, the historian Gordon Prange wrote, "The American people reeled with a mind-staggering mixture of surprise, awe, mystification, grief, humiliation, and above all cataclysmic fury." Quoted in Mueller, *War and Ideas*, p. 192.

53. It is named after Joseph P. Overton, who developed the idea.

54. "The most powerful official operates, and the most portentous decisions are taken, within a frame of reference and a climate of opinion which is of transcendent importance." Perkins, *op. cit.*, p. 186. "Opinion thus establishes limitations and constraints for foreign-policy makers like the president." Mueller, *War and Ideas*, p. 163.

55. Tocqueville thought democracies, and therefore the United States, were prone to this kind of behavior. He wrote of "the propensity that induces democracies to obey impulse rather than prudence." Alexis de Tocqueville, *Democracy in America*, New York: Vintage Books, 1945, Volume I, p. 246.

56. David Hackett Fischer traces this attitude to Scots-Irish immigrants to the United States in the eighteenth century. David Hackett Fischer, *Albion's Seed: Four British Folkways in North America*, New York: Oxford University Press, 1989, pp. 605–782. Walter Russell Mead refers to it as the "Jacksonian" tradition in American foreign policy, after President Andrew Jackson, who embodied it. Mead, *op. cit.*, Chapter 7.

57. "Although the remaining months of 1770 offered up no further violence in Boston, the angers and the hatreds that had come to the town since 1765 did not disappear. Similar feelings elsewhere in America took fresh life from the killings in Boston. The Massacre—it was called that almost immediately—compelled attention all over again to the question of what British power was doing in America." Robert Middlekauff, *The Glorious Cause: The American Revolution, 1763–1789*, New York: Oxford University Press, Second Edition, 2005, p. 212.

58. On the American response to these events, see Wood, *op. cit.*, pp. 641, 643.

59. Howe, *op. cit.*, pp. 736–737.

60. Frederick Merk, "Dissent in the Mexican War," in Samuel Eliot Morison, Frederick Merk, and Frank Freidel, editors, *Dissent in Three American Wars*, Cambridge, Massachusetts: Harvard University Press, 1970, pp. 35–37, 43–45; Mandelbaum, *The Four Ages of American Foreign Policy*, p. 94.

61. "The news [of Fort Sumter] galvanized the North. On April 15 Lincoln issued a proclamation calling 75,000 militiamen into national service ... The response from free states was overwhelming. War meetings in every city and village cheered the flag and vowed vengeance on traitors." McPherson, *op. cit.*, p. 274.

62. Kagan, *The Ghost at the Feast*, p. 39.

63. "'Remember the Maine, to hell with Spain' became a popular rallying cry ... Theater audiences wept, stamped their feet and cheered when patriotic songs were played. Jingoes wrapped themselves in flags and demanded war." Herring, *op. cit.*, p. 313. See also Osgood, *op. cit.*, p. 43.

64. Kagan, *The Ghost at the Feast*, pp. 120–128; Osgood, *op. cit.*, pp. 122, 226. See also p. 65.

65. See p. 33.

66. Mandelbaum, *The Four Ages of American Foreign Policy*, p. 250.

67. *Ibid.*, pp. 199–200; Herring, *op. cit.*, pp. 519–521. "In May 1940, before the Germans entered Paris, two-thirds of Americans polled believed it was more important for the United States to stay out of the war than to aid Britain if it increased the risk that the United States could be pulled in. By October 1940, after the fall of France, a majority of Americans believed it was more important to aid Britain than to stay out of the war. Only on the question of whether the United States should itself declare war were majorities consistently opposed." Kagan, *The Ghost at the Feast*, p. 406.

68. Ernest R. May, *"Lessons" of the Past: The Use and Misuse of History in American Foreign Policy*, New York: Oxford University Press, 1973, pp. 52, 80–81; Patterson, *Grand Expectations*, pp. 210–214.

69. Herring, *op. cit.*, p. 691; Patterson, *Grand Expectations*, pp. 418–420. Sputnik also created the climate of opinion in which John F. Kennedy was able to win election as president while asserting that the United States was falling behind the Soviet Union in their global competition. See p. 108.

70. An encounter between American ships and North Vietnamese forces in the Gulf of Tonkin off the coast of Vietnam in August 1964 led to a congressional resolution authorizing President Lyndon Johnson to "take all necessary measures to repel any armed attack" by communist North Vietnam. Herring, *op. cit.*, pp. 738–739. The episode did not have a galvanizing impact on the American public, however, and the resolution did not amount to a formal declaration of war.

71. Mandelbaum, *The Four Ages of American Foreign Policy*, pp. 342–343. The Soviet invasion of Afghanistan also repeated the experience of Sputnik in that it helped the challenger, in this case Ronald Reagan, win the presidency while promising a more vigorous prosecution of the Cold War, which paved the way for a significant increase in defense spending. See p. 108.

72. Mandelbaum, *The Four Ages of American Foreign Policy*, pp. 385–387; Patterson, *Restless Giant*, p. 233.

73. Mueller, *War and Ideas*, p. 202.

74. Melvyn P. Leffler, *Confronting Saddam Hussein: George W. Bush and the Invasion of Iraq*, New York: Oxford University Press, 2023, pp. 85–91; Mandelbaum, *The Four Ages of American Foreign Policy*, pp. 428–430.

75. Mandelbaum, *Mission Failure*, p. 230; Mandelbaum, *The Four Ages of American Foreign Policy*, p. 429.

76. Kagan, *The Ghost at the Feast*, pp. 105–106.

77. Mandelbaum, *The Four Ages of American Foreign Policy*, p. 161.

78. "[T]he 1930s, especially the decade's later years, and the period between the outbreak of war in Europe and American entry into it at the end of 1941, provide a vivid illustration of the singularly democratic character of American foreign policy. Public opinion circumscribed that policy more narrowly than the president wished." *Ibid.*, p. 198.

79. Herring, *op. cit.*, p. 503; Kennedy, *op. cit.*, pp. 387, 390.

80. "Iron-toothed insistence on full payment of the Allied war debts thus became not only a financial issue but a political and psychological issue as well, a totem of disgust with corrupt Europe, of regret at having intervened in the European war." Kennedy, *op. cit.*, p. 73. See also Osgood, *op. cit.*, p. 331.

81. "Scientific surveys of public opinion were just coming into use, and a February 1937 poll indicated that a stunning 95 percent of Americans agreed that the nation should not participate in any future war." Herring, *op. cit.*, p. 504. In the second half of the 1930s, Congress passed a series of laws known as the "Neutrality Acts" limiting what the United States could do for belligerent parties to any war. Kupchan, *op. cit.*, pp. 279–280; Kennedy, *op. cit.*, p. 400.

82. Mandelbaum, *The Four Ages of American Foreign Policy*, p. 311; Mueller, *War and Ideas*, pp. 185, 209.

83. Mandelbaum, *The Four Ages of American Foreign Policy*, p. 349; Herring, *op. cit.*, p. 868.

84. Mueller, *War and Ideas*, p. 218. The 1991 Gulf War maintained public support because it ended relatively rapidly and with few American casualties. Had it proven more costly, it almost certainly would have lost popularity. John Mueller, *Policy and Opinion in the Gulf War*, Chicago: University of Chicago Press, 1994, pp. xv, xvii.

85. Mueller, *War and Ideas*, pp. 194, 209.

86. Jay Solomon, *The Iran Wars: Spy Games, Bank Battles, and the Secret Deals That Reshaped the Middle East*, New York: Random House, 2016, pp. 288–289.

87. A historically important political initiative took place during the Revolutionary War as well, although it did not come from the president (there was none at the time) and did not aim mainly to influence domestic public opinion. The Continental Congress declared the thirteen colonies to be an independent country on July 4, 1776, in order, among other purposes, to win support from the European powers for the American war against the British Empire. "By declaring independence, the Americans hoped to make themselves a more attractive recipient of European assistance by showing their seriousness and determination." Mandelbaum, *The Four Ages of American Foreign Policy*, p. 29.

88. Howe, *op. cit.*, p. 803.

89. *Ibid.*, pp. 752, 797; Merk, *op. cit.*, pp. 58–59.

90. Howe, *op. cit.*, p. 806.

91. The president was personally opposed to slavery, believing it to be morally wrong although he had not entered office committed to abolishing it. He also wanted to complicate the war effort of the Confederacy, which was fighting to maintain slavery, and to enlist freed slaves in the Union's military efforts. McPherson, *op. cit.*, pp. 504, 567.

92. *Ibid.*, p. 510.

93. *Ibid.*, p. 567.

94. Kennedy, *op. cit.*, p. 579.

95. "About 500,000 Americans remained loyal to Britain between 1775 and 1783, and perhaps as many as 80,000 of them left their homes to take refuge in England, Canada, Nova Scotia, and the West Indies." Middlekauff, *op. cit.*, pp. 563–564.

96. Samuel Eliot Morison, "Dissent in the War of 1812," in Morison, Merk, and Freidel, *op. cit.*, p. 3. "If the war and its economic hardships had dragged on much longer, the federal government, the Constitution, and the Republican Party might not have survived intact." Howe, *op. cit.*, p. 73.

97. Howe, *op. cit.*, pp. 68–69.

98.   See p. 105.

99.   Howe, *op. cit.*, pp. 762–770.

100. McPherson, *op. cit.*, pp. 493–494, 591–592.

101. Kagan, *The Ghost at the Feast*, pp. 50, 84. On the opposition to empire in the wake of the war more generally, see Warren Zimmerman, *First Great Triumph: How Five Americans Made Their Country a World Power*, New York: Farrar, Straus and Giroux, 2002, pp. 329–345.

102. Olson, *op. cit.*, pp. 224–227, 232–238.

103. A fourth war, in Afghanistan, followed a similar trajectory, although public opposition to that war never became as politically forceful as in the other three cases.

104. The inverse relationship between casualties and public support is a theme of Mueller, *War, Presidents, and Public Opinion*. See, for example, pp. 59–61.

CONCLUSION

1.   See Michael Mandelbaum, *The Ideas That Conquered the World: Peace, Democracy, and Free Markets in the Twenty-First Century*, New York: PublicAffairs, 2002.

2.   "In 1900, only ten countries were democracies. By mid-century the number had increased to thirty, and twenty-five years later it remained there. By 2005, 119 of the world's 190 countries were democracies." Michael Mandelbaum, *Democracy's Good Name: The Rise and Risks of the World's Most Popular Form of Government*, New York: PublicAffairs, 2007, p. xi.

3.   Ian Morris, *War: What Is It Good For? Conflict and the Progress of Civilization from Primates to Robots*, New York: Farrar, Straus and Giroux, 2014, pp. 1–2.

4.   John Mueller, *Retreat from Doomsday: The Obsolescence of Major War*, New York: Basic Books, 1989, pp. 217–219; Azar Gat, *The Causes of War and the Spread of Peace: But Will War Rebound?* New York: Oxford University Press, 2017, Chapter 6.

5.   Charles Lipson, *Reliable Partners: How Democracies Have Made a Separate Peace*, Princeton: Princeton University Press, 2003, pp. 2, 4, 6, 11; Mandelbaum, *Democracy's Good Name*, Chapter 4.

6.   "In the second half of the twentieth century, American commitments, especially to military protection for commerce and to access for other countries to American capital and American markets, were indispensable to the success of the Western economies. That success, in turn, along with communist failures, created the conditions to which Mikhail Gorbachev responded with the initiatives that led, ultimately, to the demise of communism." Michael Mandelbaum, *The Four Ages of American Foreign Policy: Weak Power, Great Power, Superpower, Hyperpower*, New York: Oxford University Press, 2022, p. 374. "The causes of the ultimate victory of the United States over the Soviet Union in the Cold War were many. It is clear, however, that among the central causes were the dynamism of the open international economy, the inability of the Soviet system to cope with this, and the pressures that this put upon the Soviet leadership to change—and ultimately to abandon—that system." James Kurth, *The American Way of Empire:*

How America Won a World—But Lost Her Way, Washington, DC: Washington Books, 2019, p. 148.

7.   Michael Mandelbaum, *The Road to Global Prosperity*, New York: Simon & Schuster, 2014, pp. 21–28.

8.   *Ibid.*, pp. 15–21.

9.   Alexis de Tocqueville, *Democracy in America*, Volume I, New York: Vintage Books, 1945, pp. 244, 243.

10. Robert Kagan, *The Ghost at the Feast: America and the Collapse of World Order, 1900–1941*, New York: Alfred A. Knopf, 2023, pp. 434, 441.

11. Mandelbaum, *The Four Ages of American Foreign Policy*, p. 272.

12. *Ibid.*, p. 343; George C. Herring, *From Colony to Superpower: U.S. Foreign Relations Since 1776*, New York: Oxford University Press, 2008, p. 720.

13. Mandelbaum, *The Four Ages of American Foreign Policy*, p. 343.

14. "The history of the United States has been one of repeated surprises, not only at the behavior of others but at the behavior of the United States in response to the actions of others." Robert Kagan, *Dangerous Nation: America and the World, 1600–1898*, London: Atlantic Books, 2006, p. 5.

15. The United States did not withdraw its troops from Korea as it did from Vietnam and Iraq, (although some did subsequently return there), but the public made clear its strong desire to end the fighting, and thus the ongoing increase of American casualties, on the Korean peninsula.

16. Daniel Kahneman, *Thinking, Fast and Slow*, New York: Farrar, Straus and Giroux, 2011, pp. 345–346.

17. John Lewis Gaddis, *We Now Know: Rethinking Cold War History*, New York: Oxford University Press, 1997, pp. 200–201, 288–289.